ANCHORING AND MOORING TECHNIQUES ILLUSTRATED

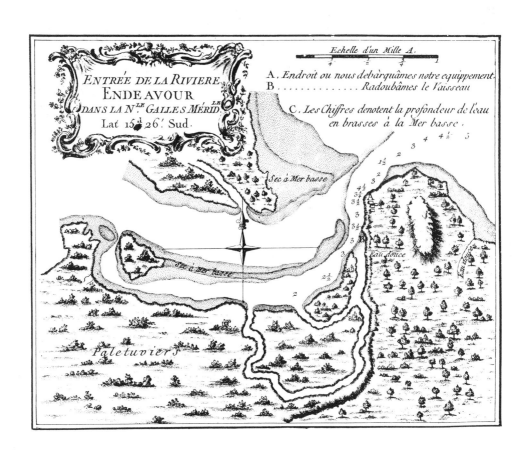

Echelle d'un Mille A.

ENTRÉE DE LA RIVIERE
ENDEAVOUR
DANS LA N.LE GALLES MÉRID.LE
Lat 15.d 26.' Sud.

A. Endroit ou nous debàrquâmes notre equippement.
B .... Radoubâmes le Vaisseau

C. Les Chiffres denotent la profondeur de l'eau
en brasses à la Mer basse.

Sec à Mer basse

Eau douce

Paletuviers

ANCHORING AND MOORING TECHNIQUES ILLUSTRATED

ALAIN GRĒE
translated by Mark Brackenbury

ADLARD COLES LIMITED

Adlard Coles Ltd
Granada Publishing Ltd
8 Grafton Street, London W1X 3LA

First published in France under the title *Mouillage Equipement & Technique*
by Voiles/Gallimard in 1981
First published in Great Britain by
Granada Publishing in Adlard Coles Ltd 1984

British Library Cataloguing in Publication Data
Grée, Alain
Anchoring and mooring techniques illustrated.
1. Anchorage   2. Yachts and yachting
I. Title   II. Mouillage equipement &
technique. *English*
623.88'8   VM791

ISBN 0-229-11702-3

Typesetting and origination by
CG Graphic Services, Aylesbury, Bucks
Printed and bound in Great Britain by
R. J. Acford, Chichester, Sussex

CONTENTS

1 Part One
ANCHORIN
EQUIPMEN'

Anchors

It isn't a real cruise unless, maybe just for a night, maybe for longer, we can drop our hook into the sheltered waters of some quiet anchorage and take our ease. But look: over there on the horizon the white horses are already beginning to form. Will the anchor hold?

importance of a boat's anchors their related gear is absolutely damental. The breakdown of an tronic wind indicator, a rip in spinnaker or a log that refuses record: this sort of problem ly has catastrophic results. But horing is quite another matter. ragging anchor, a shackle com-open or an anchor warp parting being chafed through by a rp edge of rock, and the boat be driven ashore in seconds. In weather, such an occurrence ally means the loss of the boat, sometimes that of the crew.

my wanderings, I have en-ntered many anchorage prob-s, in different circumstances in wind strengths varying from 70 knots. In the Aegean during *eltemi*, I was obliged to use e anchors – two kedges backed the bower – before the rocks ch threatened my stern could persuaded to keep their dis-e. In the Grenadines, had it not n for the providential presence rock pinnacle around which we aged one morning to fasten last warp, my boat *Pitcairn* ld have been driven straight a reef of brown coral. Off la in the Strait of Messina, I e even had to keep the diesel ing all night to avoid being shed against the hull of an ressive trawler. This was in a

squall that attained force ten while veering through 180°, and in the middle of a fleet of fishing boats, more than half of which had been lying with their anchors foul of my chain since the beginning of the squall. I carry four heavy anchors aboard, each with its own cable, and I also carry over 100 fathom of 20mm diameter floating warp. Hav-ing used them regularly, I consider them to be indispensable for a boat that is going to sail far from her home port, if one wants to be able to cope with unexpected crises at any moment – and they do happen often.

Even 'coastal cruising' (and that, let's face it, is the most dangerous place to be sailing) for just a few weeks a year doesn't mean that you may not be confronted with a sud-den squall. It can strike at any time: in port, lying to a stern anchor, in an open anchorage among lurking reefs, or just simply through rudder failure upwind of a menacing lee shore. It is in these circumstances, so common as to be positively banal, that the quality of the anchoring equipment available aboard shows its true worth. Be-cause there are no half measures with an anchor: either it holds or it drags. It's up to you to make sure that yours only understands the former verb. Nothing is more essential.

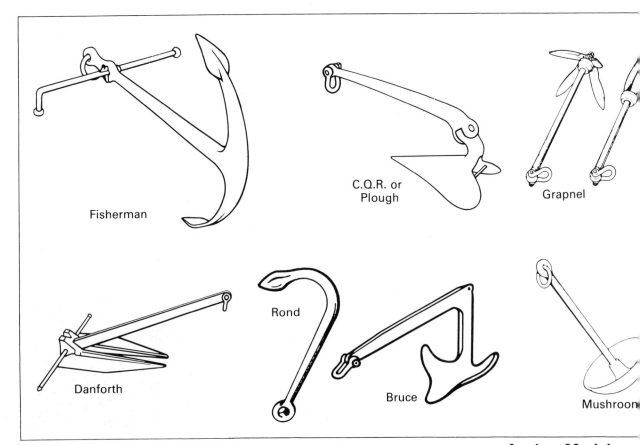

Fisherman

C.Q.R. or Plough

Grapnel

Rond

Danforth

Bruce

Mushroom

Portrait of an Anchor

An anchor is a metal instrument designed to dig into the bottom, with the object of holding the boat to which it is attached by a cable, and preventing it from moving under the influence of wind or current. That is a beautiful definition, which may well set out the precise function of this vital accessory, but entirely fails to mention the difficulties that can attend its use. They are legion! The first is choosing the right one. Obviously the essential quality for an anchor is holding power. For a given wind strength, this will depend on five main interlinked factors:

- design of the anchor
- its weight
- nature of the bottom
- composition of the cable
- length of the scope (1).

This combination of factors requires a great deal of thought, especially when the wind is blowing violently. Theoretically, as always, the solution seems simple: in the light of the old sailors' saying 'Ground tackle can never be too heavy', all you have to do is anchor a little yacht with an aircraft-carrier anchor, and you will be sure that it will hold. But the real problem arises from the fact that on our boats we have to avoid excessive weight, and that there is not much room for stowage and only limited power available through the windlass (if there is one at all), so in practice we have to limit both the weight and the size of the anchors we carry.

Thus, our anchors must have maximum holding power for a minimum of weight and volume: hence the necessity to choose the best performing models.

Anchor Models

Anchors used aboard yachts ca classed in four main types, with its own advantages and ings.

- Stock anchors
- Plough anchors and Bruce
- Danforth-type anchors
- Grapnels.

The Plough and Danforth-anchors require the most det attention, since these are the t most commonly found on mo yachts.

(1) The scope is the length of anchc cable that has been veered. It varies with the depth of water, strength of wind, nature of bottom and composition (all chain or chain an rope) of the cable.

...ft, the anchors most commonly seen
... *boats today. Right, very few yachts*
...n afford the space and weight to
...rry this sort of massive winch and
...uipment.

The Stock anchor
(...isherman, Admiralty pattern etc)

...is is the classic anchor of earlier
...ys, and was once used by vessels
... all sizes. Its long survival is
...plained by its performance: no
...her anchor equals it in holding
...ility. But it is seen on few yachts
...day, because it is cumbersome
...d difficult to handle.

...escription. There are three main
...rts. At one end of the shank are
...e arms, which are slightly curved
...d end in triangular flukes, and at
...e other is a stock, set at right
...gles to the line of the arms. The
...ock is usually collapsible to make
...owage easier.

...dvantages. The Stock anchor is
...ten the only one that will hold in
...nse weed, which is an important
...ality on coasts, where weed is
...mmon. The reliability with which
...akes hold is notable, owing to its
...ng narrow arms, one of which is
...ways pointing straight down-
...rds as it is drawn across the
...ttom. (This is dependent on the
...ain used being of adequate
...eight: we will discuss this in the
...xt chapter.) It is in fact the weight
...the chain that holds the stock flat
...the bottom, ensuring that one of
...e arms is held in a position to dig
...)

Disadvantages. There are two: (1)
the heavy weight which is required
to achieve the same holding power
(weed excepted) as the high performance CQR or Danforth types;
(2) the encumbrance of the
opposed arms and stock, which
makes it difficult to stow on the
stemhead, on deck or in a locker. As
for the collapsible models, the time
needed to set them up excludes
them from use as a main, or even
secondary anchor, and one must
also always be aware of the risk
with this type that if the stock
retaining pin comes out, the stock
will fold and the anchor become
useless. One final snag, and not the
least, is the risk that after a change
of wind or tide the chain may foul
the stock or the upper arm of the
anchor, causing it to drag and making it difficult or impossible for it to
re-engage.

Uses. Although seldom seen on
modern yachts, a Fisherman can
prove itself invaluable in one special situation – as an emergency
anchor in severe conditions, when
the other anchors carried have
failed to hold. This is on condition
that it is oversized, and that if the
bottom is sandy, it can be allowed
plenty of distance to dig in. Only a
collapsible model would be practicable, kept in reserve at the bottom
of a locker, in the hope that it would
never be needed.

*Perhaps the most efficient anchor
designed, the name CQR is der
from the English word 'sec
Beware of inferior copies, as
design and quality of materials
workmanship are crit*

The Plough anchor (CQR Bruce etc.)

Designed in England in 1933 by Professor (later Sir) Geoffrey Taylor, the CQR was originally intended for use on flying boats. This throws interesting light on the reason why so much research went into it, as the importance of weight-saving in aeronautics is obvious. Its arrival was greeted enthusiastically by the yachtsmen of the period, who almost unanimously recognised its remarkable efficiency:

'It is a great advance on existing types. Its slightly un-nautical appearance may cause a few eyebrows to be raised, but it is none the less true that its holding power for a given weight is more than five times that of an ordinary anchor.' (H. Dervin, 1935.)

Things have hardly changed since then: the CQR (a phonetic corruption of the word 'secure') is still considered by yachtsmen to be, if not the perfect anchor, at least the best available today.

Description Two symmetrical blades, resembling a double ploughshare, are hinged at the end of the shank in such a way that, when the anchor is pulled by the chain attached to the ring, the shape of the blades tends to drive the point into the bottom. The pull of the chain produces this result no matter what the position of the anchor, which is an important fea-

ture. The reinforcing strut between the ears of the plough blades can be used for the attachment of a tripping line. The hinging of the head to the shank provides a degree of flexibility which can ease stowage problems, whether on deck or in a locker.

Advantages Excellent holding on all bottoms except very thick weed. Ratio of holding power to weight very favourable, allowing the use of a lighter anchor to achieve the required efficiency. Also, its very structure eliminates the risk of fouling the chain on an arm or stock, which was a common event in the old days when only Stock anchors were in use. Note also the regularity with which it takes hold, even after it has dragged (in contrast to Danforth types, which tend to have difficulty in getting a grip if once they lose their first hold). In my view this is the most important advantage of the CQR: its readiness to dig in a second time after dragging. (Although they seldom do drag.)

Disadvantages The large surface of the blades tends to make the anchor slide over the surface of the weed which carpets some types of bottom. This is a problem also met with Danforth types for the same reasons: only a Fisherman can force its point through thick weed and get a grip in the mud or sand beneath. But this failing is usually made up for by the CQR's high speed in taking hold when the

chance offers. Unless there is room to fall back (dangers cl astern in an anchorage or harbor the movement astern usually st after a short distance, when anchor catches on a projection digs into some providential cle ing in the weed.

Another criticism: cumbro ness. This matters little for the m anchor, which is more and m often stowed on the stem-h roller while at sea, but does aff secondary anchors. It is still minor fault in comparision with importance of the job it does, a to get complete security one m be prepared to make a few s rifices. After all, the whole art sailing depends upon a long ser of compromises!

s At the risk of upsetting the ntors and makers of other s, I must say that I think the ities of Plough anchors make n the most suitable type for the n anchor on a yacht. This is e out by their world-wide ularity. Safety first.

however, the design of the t for some reason makes the of a Plough as the main anchor ossible, and no modification is rticable, at least equip yourself a CQR as a second anchor, so it can always be called upon if main anchor begins to drag.

don't say 'If there's anyone rd at the time': a boat should er be left untended on a single ior. Not even for ten minutes.

The Bruce anchor

This relative newcomer to the ranks of Plough type anchors was developed for oil rigs, and the makers claim performance in excess of any other anchor of the same weight, though the figures later in this book do not altogether bear this out. They also claim good performance when the scope is very short, which seems likely in view of the unusual shape, a curved ploughshare with three blunt flukes, attached rigidly to an L–shaped shank. It is perhaps the most awkward of all anchors to stow, and in my opinion this factor is not compensated for by any material advantage in holding capability, certainly not at the relatively lightweight end of the market where our tests were made.

Once the anchor is ready to let go at the skipper's order, the crew has time for a final moment's relaxation before entering harbour.
Below, a 45 lb Bruce.

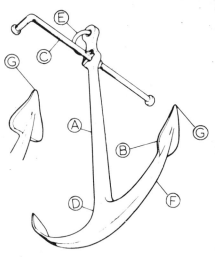

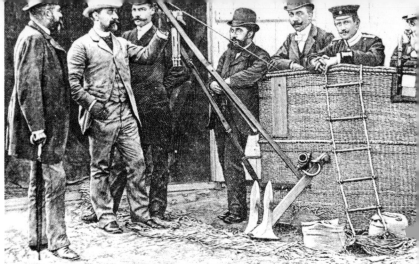

The principal parts of an anchor. A, shank. B, flukes which dig into the ground. C, stock which stabilises the anchor. D, crown which connects the main parts. E, ring to which the cable is bent. F, arms. G, bill.

Danforth and similar types

There is no satisfactory word in the English language to describe this group, known in French as *ancres à bascule* (from *bascule*, see-saw), but this is the group whose blades are hinged to the shank with restricted movement, so that whichever way the anchor falls the points will bear down on the bottom. The Danforth (developed in America by

R. Danforth in 1939) has a stock, but many others of this type do not. In France, the designs used are mainly the Danforth, Fob and Britany, and they are the main rivals to the CQR.

Description Two wide blades with more or less narrow points are hinged so that they can deflect to an angle of about 30° from the line of the shank, but no further. There may or may not be a stock running out from the line of the base of the blades.

Advantages The holding power varies with design, but is always mediocre on weedy bottoms. The greatest advantage is in their ease of stowage: the hinges allow them to lie completely flat. As with the CQR, there is also little risk of fouling on the chain.

They operate as follows: dragged down by its heavy crown, the anchor falls to the bottom and lies flat. As soon as the strain comes on the cable, the blades hinge downwards and the points are forced into the bottom. The heavy weight built into the crown adds to the pressure, and the stronger the pull the deeper the blades will bury themselves. There are circumstances, however, in which the massive crown can prevent the penetration of the points, especially as the speed at which the boat is falling back builds up. This problem will be examined later, in the chapter on experimental trials.

To combat this important fa[ ] some types (Britany and Fob[ ] for example) use blades of redu[ ] width. This improvement also [ ] duces the risk of dragging while [ ] anchor is pivoting horizontally [ ] the boat swings. It is certainly t[ ] that narrow-bladed types (D[ ] forth, Fob-HP, Britany) h[ ] markedly better than the w[ ] bladed versions that are to a la[ ] extent responsible for the p[ ] reputation of this group.

Disadvantages Danforth-t[ ] anchors are well known for t[ ] tendency to refuse to regain h[ ] once they have dragged, particu[ ] ly if the boat is by then movin[ ] some speed, which is usually [ ] case in such circumstances. [ ] therefore essential to choose h[ ] efficiency types to reduce as fa[ ] possible the risk of dragging.

Personally, I remain convin[ ] that to obtain equivalent hold[ ] power to a CQR, a substanti[ ] heavier Danforth or similar anc[ ] must be used. And one must h[ ] the capability (muscular or mec[ ] nical) of getting it back aboa[ ] because fifteen fathoms of ch[ ] hanging down vertically with[ ] heavy anchor at the end of i[ ] quite a weight!

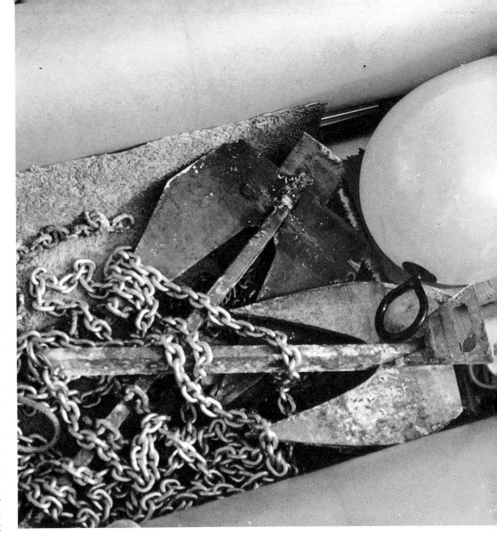

...e crew of Phénix, *left, before her ...arture on 4th December 1894. One ...urprised to find a Danforth-type ...hor at this period, and even more ...o learn that* Phénix *was not a boat ...a balloon! A balloon (not always ...gible) which that day attained an ...ude of over 30,000 feet before ...ning to anchor' 194 miles from her ...ting point. Below left, a Danforth ...h a stainless steel chain. Right, a ...tany and a Fob-HP.*

...es All experienced users (start-
with Eric Tabarly) are unani-
...us in claiming better holding for
... CQR. If your deck plan cannot
...e a CQR as main anchor, you will
...ve to make do with the Danforth
...e your builder has supplied.
...'s hope it is heavy enough.
...nerwise, use this anchor as a
...dge, not as the main one. The
...vival of your boat, and her crew,
...y depend upon it.
...Of course, these remarks apply to
...nforth-type anchors actually
...ailable today. The trials men-
...ned above confirm my reserva-
...ns about these anchors: even on
...andy bottom, the holding power
...he Fob-HP and Britany remained
... below that of the CQR (about
...%) and they pulled out several
...es, while the CQR kept up a
...nstant resistance. No doubt it is
...s lack of power and reliability
...t led the inventor of the Britany,
...nand Colin, to go on trying to
...prove his original model. He
...st be commended for his con-
...uing research in this area. He has
...ently brought out two pro-
...ypes, one in light alloy rather
...n steel, and a version with fold-
... lateral stabilisers. These two
...ations obtained spectacular re-
...ts in tests organised in October
...30 by the inventor, but the condi-
...ns under which the tests were
...ried out were too specialised to
...rmit the results to be considered
... reliable guide to performance
...der general conditions. The fact

remains that the great reliability of holding provided by the CQR and the Bruce appears far superior to that of Danforth types. For the moment, we can only note these results, until we can try the new anchors on varying bottoms and under differing conditions. And that will need some time.

On these two pages we examine the principal characteristics of the three types of anchor most commonly used on modern yachts: the CQR, a Danforth type (Simpson-Lawrence's S-L Clyde anchor) and the Bruce.

1 CQR

Weight		Length	Length of Plough	Width of Plough
7 kg	15 lb	26 in	13 in	10 in
9 kg	20 lb	30 in	15 in	11 in
11 kg	25 lb	32 in	17 in	12 in
15 kg	35 lb	38 in	19 in	13 in
20 kg	45 lb	41 in	20 in	15 in
27 kg	60 lb	43 in	22 in	16 in
34 kg	75 lb	47 in	26 in	18 in
45 kg	100 lb	47 in	26 in	18 in

2 DANFORTH-TYPE (S-L CLYDE)

Weight		Length (fluke)	Length (shank)	Width (stock)
2·27 kg	5 lb	13 in	8¾ in	12 in
4·55 kg	10 lb	19⅝ in	14¼ in	18 in
6·82 kg	15 lb	23⅝ in	15¾ in	21½ in
9·07 kg	20 lb	29⅛ in	19¼ in	26 in
11·30 kg	25 lb	29⅛ in	19¼ in	26 in

3 BRUCE

Weight		Depth	Length	Width
2 kg	4·4 lb	7·2 in	14·3 in	9·7 in
5 kg	11·0 lb	9·4 in	18·5 in	12·4 in
7½ kg	16·5 lb	10·7 in	20·9 in	14·2 in
10 kg	22·0 lb	11·5 in	23·0 in	15·2 in
15 kg	33·0 lb	13·5 in	25·8 in	17·0 in
20 kg	44·0 lb	14·6 in	27·6 in	18·0 in

1

CQR Anchor

This Ploughshare anchor has often been imitated but nev equalled, for three reasons: (1) the components are oft cast rather than drop forged, which fails to provide t necessary strength; (2) the anchors are not properly b lanced, and (3) the angles of attack are not accurate reproduced. The whole principle of the anchor's operatio without which performance can be seriously affected, d pends on the balance of the ploughshare with respect to t shank. The weight of the metal must bear down on the poi of attack of the ploughshare: this can be proved by pulli the anchor along for a few inches balanced upright on i blades. The least unevenness should make the plough fa over to one side or the other.

Some users (and imitators) wrongly suppose that t ploughshare operates vertically. This is quite wrong: the be results only come when it has fallen over onto its side.

2

The Danforth Anchor

Danforth has been successfully reproduced in many
ntries outside its native USA, perhaps because the design
ss complex and critical than that of the CQR. It is
rtant, however, to ensure that whatever version is
en is strongly made, as when well dug in in firm holding,
t force can be required to break it out, and bent shanks or
es are not uncommon, either of which can render the
or useless. It is important to ensure also that the pivot
ates freely, as if it is stiffened by corrosion or marine
th, efficiency can be seriously impaired. If purchasing a
less type, be sure that there is a crown ring to which a
ing line can be attached, as if there is difficulty in
king out the anchor, a forward pull on a tripping line will
do this quite easily.

3

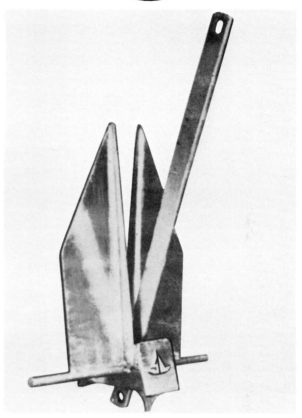

The Bruce Anchor

Developed in 1972 by Peter Bruce for the anchoring of oil
rigs, this strangely shaped anchor is designed so that it will
always land with its weight resting on one fluke. The shape
ensures that as the anchor is pulled along, this fluke digs in
and the anchor turns until the shank is uppermost and the
whole anchor buries completely. The makers claim exceptional performance, and this is undoubtedly the case with
large anchors: in the sizes used on yachts there seems to be
a tendency for the anchor to skate along the surface of some
kinds of bottom, without digging in. The extraordinary and
inflexible shape is an undoubted disadvantage.

At the bottom of Lake Nemi in the Roman countryside, two galleys from the reign of the tyrant Caligula lay for nearly two thousand years. Each was 246 feet long. After draining this ancient crater, situated at an altitude of 1300 feet, in 1931, the Italian government had them removed from the mud in which they had lain almost undamaged. The anchors which they still carried were of two different types: one, of iron with a moveable stock, was 13 feet long; the other, of wood with metal bindings and provided with a leaden stock, was as much as 16 feet long. Both were perfectly preserved.

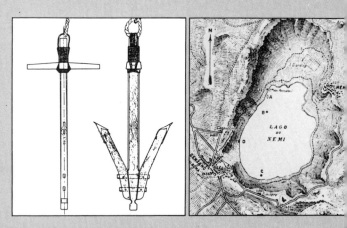

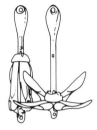

Grapnels

inly used by fishing boats, a apnel consists of a shank, at the se of which are arranged four nded arms. It used to be recomnded for use on rocky bottoms, ere the traditional Fisherman s apt to get jammed. As it would sily get a grip among jagged ks, its weight could be reduced about a third of that of a normal chor. Today, Grapnels are hardly ed except on tenders or dinghies. sily stowed folding models are ailable, perfectly designed for the they are expected to do: holda small boat in good weather a swimming or fishing party. this sort of purpose they may n be found aboard larger boats. e might consider acquiring a ger model as an occasional chor for a small yacht, for instce to restrict swinging, but never a main anchor, because of their reliable holding.

practical way of stowing a Grapnel, he bottom of a perforated plastic ket.

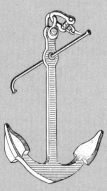

Choosing an anchor

In practice, for a cruising yacht, our choice lies between two types of anchor: Plough and Danforth type.

● **Ploughshare anchors** Undoubtedly only genuine CQRs should be considered, because of their method of manufacture (drop forged), the accurate balance of their ploughshare, and the special geometry of their angles of attack. There are many technical details which explain the better holding of the pure-bred CQR, whether made in England or elsewhere under licence.

● **Danforth types** One may consider the Danforth itself or well-constructed substitutes of known quality in materials and design: in France this would include the Britany and Fob-HP, in the UK the S-L Clyde. Note the earlier remarks about this general type of anchor.

It is important to investigate all the possibilities thoroughly before deciding on a particular preference. Test them out? I do so regularly in the case of three models, as I carry on *Pitcairn* two CQRs, an original Britany and a Fob-HP of roughly the same weight. Sailing my own boat for four or five months a year, I have clocked up enough nights at anchor for the subject to interest me by force of circumstance. Indeed, my interest has grown to a point where I actually enjoy the detailed analysis of test results. We shall come to that shortly.

1 Folding Grapnel, for holding the tender or fishing up a chain.

2 Fisherman, hardly ever used nowadays aboard modern yachts.

3 Navymat anchor: heavy crown too wide. Not recommended.

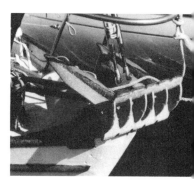

4 Dial anchor: crown too heavy: fails to hold.

5 Old 62 lb FOB: bad holder, the HP models are better.

6 Hall anchor: if it holds at all it can only be by its weight.

Bruce anchor: rather cumbersome for average performance.

10 Danforth anchor: very good holding, but the stock is cumbersome.

11 CQR ploughshare anchor: excellent holding, minimal risk of dragging.

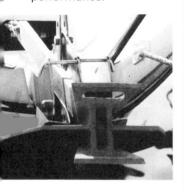

Fob-HP: a cousin of the Britany, with much the same performance.

Steel Britany anchor: good general performance, easy to stow.

 12 The heavy mob ranged in the bows: a CQR ready to drop, a Danforth in reserve and a Luke with folding stock as the last resort.

The table reproduced at the bottom of the page gives the weights of the anchors (then of the Fisherman type) recommended for yachts at the beginning of the century. These figures confirm the necessity of using heavy Fishermen if one is to be sure of good holding. They are impressive: 40 kilograms (88 lb) for a boat of 5–10 tons. (This is an extract from Treatise on Yacht Construction of 1898.) Below, old prints of a traditional anchor: (1) dug in (though not very deeply!). (2) fouled on its stock. (3) fouled over its crown.

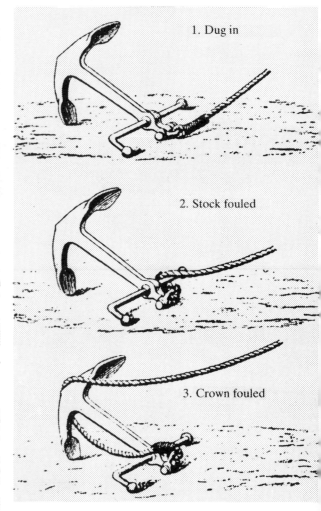

1. Dug in

2. Stock fouled

3. Crown fouled

Nombre d'ancres	1re Ancre		2e Ancre		3e Ancre		1e Ancre		Chaîne de mouillage				
	poids	Épreuve à	Poids	Épreuve	Poids	Épreuve	Poids	Épreuve	Diamètre	Longueur	Éprouvée à	Charge de rupture	Diamètre
		tonnes		tonnes									
5	2	30	15	»	»	»	»	»	9	60	2,400	3,600	
10	2	40	20	»	»	»	»	»	10	90	2,400	3,600	
20	2	50	25	»	»	»	»	»	11	90	3,500	5,250	
30	2	60	30	»	»	»	»	»	13	120	4,500	6,750	
40	2	75	40	»	»	»	30	»	14	150	4,500	8,250	
50	3	85	4,200	100	4,500	40	»	14	180	5,000	8,250		
75	3	110	4,800	150	5,500	45	»	16	180	7,000	10,500		
à 100	3	160	5,700	160	5,900	50	»	18	210	8,500	12,750		
à 125	3	180	6,150	200	6,350	50	30	»	19	210	10,120	15,120	
à 150	3	210	6,600	225	6,850	50	60	»	19	210	10,120	15,120	
à 200	4	250	7,350	260	7,550	85	4,200	40	20	240	11,900	17,800	
à 250	4	280	8,000	300	8,250	100	4,500	40	22	240	13,750	20,620	
à 300	4	325	8,750						24	270	15,800	23,700	

It was aboard Kurun, *a 33 ft cutter which could carry over 1000 square feet of sail with topsail set, that Jacques-Yves Le Toumelin achieved a magnificent circumnavigation under sail. Below, the arrival in the port of Croisic in 1952, showing his hefty Fisherman anchor.*

The fouling of fisherman-type anchors

anchor can be fouled either by ble round its stock, or when the ble fouls one of the flukes. This happen either when the anchor d cable arrive on the bottom, or er as a result of the boat swing-. The text that follows, taken m a book by J-Y Le Toumelin, strates the dangers that can re-lt from the fouling of an anchor a result of changing tidal eams. The moral is never to ve a boat unattended on a single chor, even for a few moments.

Arrival at a Pacific island often oduces three successive impressions. om out to sea, it is beautiful. Having ived at the principal village, it is rible! Then, exploring the island ay from civilization, it is beautiful! ready experienced at Tahiti, this set impressions was renewed for me at iatea.

After a short walk ashore, I sudden-felt an urge to get back aboard. uition? With a feeling of unease, I s making my way back towards the arf when someone shouted to me: 'our boat's moving!" I ran. It was e: Kurun was dragging rapidly, netimes swinging almost beam-on to wind. At a dead run, I threw myself o the pram. Sweating copiously, I nbed aboard the cutter. . . . I hurled

myself upon the windlass without wasting any more time. Weighing anchor was a long and laborious job with that scope of cable. Painfully, the chain came aboard. Several times the pawl jumped out of the ratchet, and I had to stop the crank unwinding with my leg, which cost me a good many bruises. I was exhausted, but the job had to be finished, because the cutter was still dragging and, if the wind were to shift a fraction I would be driven down onto a

coral head which I had spotted to leeward. After more than half an hour of effort, the anchor was broken out.

'Shortly afterwards, it appeared five fathoms below, with the chain fouled round both the stock and a fluke . . . the result of swinging to the stream the night before, while I slept!'

(from 'Kurun around the World', Editions Flammarion)

23

**Bay of Eupotoria
15th November 1854**

'Admiral,

'I have to give you the sorrowful news that my ship has been ashore since yesterday evening, and in view of the season I have little hope of bringing her off. This unhappy event was due to the successive failure of my four chains during the storm we have just suffered.

'All the precautions that prudence could suggest had been taken. Therefore, Admiral, I believed us to be safe until, during a violent gust from a changed direction, the starboard chain snapped clean off where it passed through the bitts. At eleven o'clock the port one, which had been regularly paid out, link by link, until there was at least 150 fathoms out, did the same. We then resorted to the starboard watch-anchor, when the chain-pawl carried away. However, a loop of the chain having jammed in the hawse hole, it held well at the seventh shackle – 126 fathoms – until ten minutes past five in the evening, when it broke as the ship pitched violently.

'The port one, now left alone, resisted for less than a minute, and it was with terror that I heard the double shock that told me that all hope of resisting the tempest was lost, and that we must resign ourselves to being driven ashore, as had already happened on this fatal day to twelve or fifteen other vessels, before my very eyes.'

Anchors in earlier years

In the days before the development of the marine engine, anchors were a far more vital part of a ship's equipment even than they are today. A modern sailing vessel, whether a yacht or commercial, will almost certainly have an auxiliary engine to help in difficult manoeuvres, but in earlier years some manoeuvres could only be achieved with the aid of an anchor, and one or more anchors were always kept ready to let go at a moment's notice, as apart from problems caused by bad weather there was always the danger of a ship getting into difficulties, for example in the entrance of a harbour, simply as a result of a change or failure of wind. Indeed a specially named 'straits anchor' was often carried secured under the bowsprit in such a way that it could be allowed to swing out and drop ahead in the event of the ship losing way while passing through a narrow channel. Many ships carried a specially heavy emergency anchor which could be brought into use in desperate conditions when the normal tackle had failed: another often used (and still useful) device in severe conditions was one for backing up the anchor. Here, a second anchor is attached by a short length of chain to the *crown* of the main anchor: this serves to hold down the main anchor as well as adding additic holding power, and as long as cable is strong enough, anchors so placed will hold m strongly than the same anch used on separate cables.

the whaler Charles W. Morgan,
in 1841, which can be admired in
open air museum at Mystic
ort. Right, plan of a roadstead
e ships anchor on range lines.

extract from *Complete Ship-*
dler by Bonnefoux, published in
first half of the nineteenth cen-
, shows the extent to which the
ains of the great sailing ships
to be at one with the natural
ents in order to manoeuvre
unmanageable vessels which
commanded. What wonderful
these old skippers had in the
of wind and current!

ry roadstead, because of the lie of
urrounding land, high or low, and
area in which it is situated, has
ys one particular direction from
h a strong wind will be most
erous. For this reason, the two
ors should be dropped on a line at
angles to the direction of the wind
to be feared, so that if that wind
chance to blow, each anchor will
vorking and contributing to the
y of the ship. In Brest, for exam-
the anchors are dropped southeast
northwest, because there the most
erous winds are from the south-
; also, the starboard anchor must
e one laid out to the northwest, so
if the ship turns to face a southwest
d she will present her bow without
sing the cables. It has also been
ed that these gales generally end
eering to a stiff northwest breeze
squalls, that the flood stream,
ing from the open side of the
our, is accompanied by more swell
that of the ebb, and that it is
erous to drag either towards the
or to the west.'

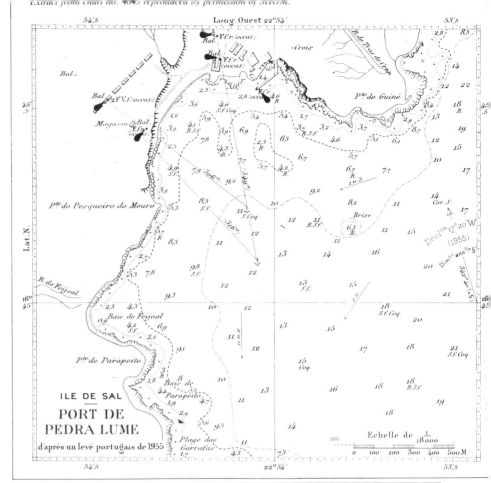

ILE DE SAL
—
PORT DE
PEDRA LUME

d'après un levé portugais de 1955

Long. Ouest 22°54'

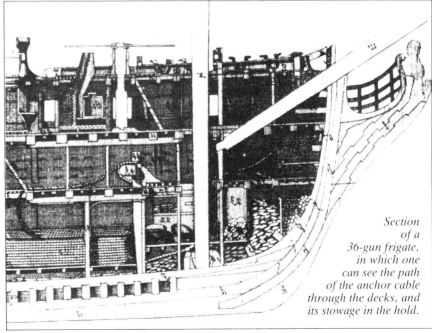

Section
of a
36-gun frigate,
in which one
can see the path
of the anchor cable
through the decks, and
its stowage in the hold.

27

Anchor chains and warps

The tragic report from which we have just read some extracts (page 25) was addressed to Vice-Admiral Hamelin by Commandant Jehenne of the vessel *Henri IV*. It demonstrates that even the heaviest of chains can, under the assault of violent weather, snap like pack thread. In spite of the technical advances that have been made since then, this should encourage us to choose our anchoring equipment with the greatest care. Not only the anchors; the chains and warps which attach us to them deserve the same attention. On their strength depends the force with which we can be held: on their number the security of the boat.

Composition of an anchor cable

Anchor cables will take various forms according to the size of the boat, the equipment available for raising the anchor, and whether it is a main or a secondary cable.

There are two possibilities: entirely chain, or a cable composed partly of chain and partly of rope. An inexperienced owner might scratch his head over these choices, but in practice the decisions make themselves, as chain cables and mixed cables each have their own individual uses. Some countries have detailed regulations governing the anchor gear that must be carried aboard pleasure craft.

All-chain cable

There can be no doubt: whatever the size of the boat, the *main* cable should be wholly chain, galvanised and conforming with the statutory or advisory regulations of the country concerned. This should go without saying if the chain is supplied by a chandler or boatyard. This chain, known as chain cable because an anchor line has always been a cable in English, is 'calibrated'. This means that its links have a regularity of shape that ensures that they will fit without any problems into the gipsy of a windlass, a characteristic not shared by chains of less elevated origin! (We owe the invention of anchor chains to Captain Samuel Brown, RN, who on the suggestion of Cook and Bougainville put chain aboard *HMS Penelope* in 1809, as a replacement for the fragile hemp rope cables that had been in use up to that time.)

Why all-chain?

There are three principal reasons:

(1) The heavy weight of this me[ ] cable ensures that the anc[ ] achieves its best coefficient [ ] penetration because the pull [ ] ways comes horizontally.

(2) Resistance to abrasion, imp[ ]tant in bad weather. A rope ca[ ] will chafe at points of strain [ ] friction, of which there are seve[ ] between the deck and the anch[ ] cleats or samson post, fairlea[ ] stemhead fittings, abrasive rock[ ] coral on the bottom. One must a[ ] take account of the possibility [ ] accidental cutting caused by sh[ ] rocks or a carelessly handled pr[ ]eller (this happened to me at My[ ]nos ten years ago, upwind fr[ ] some unhealthy-looking rocks, a[ ] I do not intend to forget the less[ ] An all-chain cable gives a compl[ ] guarantee against this sort of n[ ] adventure.

(3) The elasticity provided by t[ ] great length of chain preve[ ] snubbing caused by swell, squal[ ] swinging. This is important, as [ ] reduces the risk of gear failure [ ] dragging. Believe me, the sho[ ] that can be felt on such occasic[ ] can be quite unbelievable. T[ ] weight of the chain itself is usua[ ] enough to prevent violent sn[ ]bing, without the need to resort [ ] cable-weights.

VI 5452

When racing, the interests of good distribution of weight, and the nee[d] for an uncluttered stem and forede[ck] mean that anchoring gear tends to [be] kept to the bare essentials, and stow[ed] amidships.

In the first place, to weight [the] fore part of the cable, so that [the] pull on the anchor comes m[ore] horizontally. This is essential if [the] anchor is to hold well; after all, [all] that is needed to break out [the] anchor is to raise the rear of [the] stock by hauling on the cable fr[om] above. Secondly, the presence [of] this length of chain reduces [the] chafing on roughnesses on the b[ot] tom that occurs when a rope [is] attached directly to an anchor.

This is not all. The inertia res[ult] ing from the weight of the length [of] chain, as well as keeping the dir[ec] tion of traction horizontal, also c[on] siderably reduces the lateral stra[in] on the anchor caused by the ve[er] ing of the boat on the surface. A[nd] it is generally when the tens[ion] changes from its original direct[ion] that dragging occurs, particula[rly] with Danforth-type anchors. W[ith] the two blades not work[ing] together, but tending to pi[vot] round one of them, the anchor [will] break out (in these circumstan[ces] the CQR shows better resistance[, or] at least is more likely to re-enga[ge]. This is why the chain part o[f a] mixed cable should be as long [as] possible, and whatever happe[ns] must not be omitted.

These three advantages should persuade every skipper to equip his main anchor with an all-chain cable, even though nylon may be more pleasant to handle. On it will rest the safety of his boat and crew.

Disadvantage. There is only one, a side-effect of one of the advantages: its weight. A nuisance for those seeking extremes of lightness or those with a mania about weight distribution (and they have a point, as anchor gear is normally stowed right forward), this problem is above all noticeable in its effect on the effort needed to recover the anchor. Fifteen fathom of 9·5 mm

(⅜") chain with a 45 lb anchor at the end is heavy: getting on for 200 lb all up. But the equipment on modern boats makes this operation much easier; let's be honest, apart from stripped-down racing boats there are very few boats large enough to need gear of that weight which do not carry a winch — manual, electric or hydraulic.

Mixed chain and nylon

The mixed cable is composed of a short length of chain shackled to the anchor ring, and completed by fifty fathoms or so of rope. Why does one put this length of chain between the rope and the anchor?

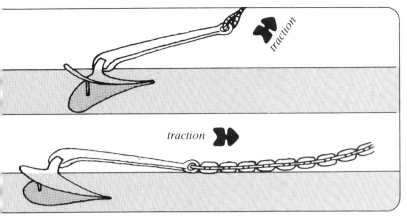

Role of the chain:

● *Rope attached directly to the anchor ring (or insufficient length of chain): the pull is directed towards the surface. There is a constant tendency to break out the anchor.*

traction

● *Chain between the rope and the anchor: the pull comes horizontally, thanks to the presence of the chain, kept on the bottom by its weight. The anchor therefore tends to bury itself deeper.*

traction

A quick calculation shows the considerable weight of anchoring gear. On a 39 ft boat:

● *Three 35 lb anchors*

● *50 fathoms of 9·5 mm (³⁄₈″) chain, and two 12 fathom lengths: at about 10 lb per fathom, say 750 lb*

● *75 fathoms of 18 mm diameter warp at about 14 oz to the fathom, say 65 lb. Grand total, 920 lb.*

A racing vessel may consider reducing these amounts in the search for maximum performance, but for cruising it cannot be reduced without imperilling the safety of the boat.

Measurement and testing of chain

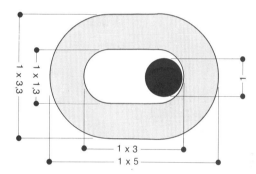

The diagram shows a typical link of marine quality chain cable, all measurements being given as multiples of the diameter measured through any part of an individual link. Precise test requirements vary, of course, in different countries, but they are usually carefully defined and cover such questions as breaking strain, degree of stretch under strain, strain under which measurable temporary/permanent distortion is suffered and (most important for marine use) regularity of shape and size and lack of galvanising nodules, to ensure the chain's trouble-free passage through a winch or windlass.

Having hauled up the anchor, the warp must be conscientiously coiled down ready to be let run freely through the stemhead at any moment, preferably without getting a large loop round the pulpit, as in this picture.

Length of the anchor cable

As a result of some curious reasoning, French regulations lay down that every anchor cable should be at least five times the length of the boat. This means that for an 18-footer, and there are plenty of cruising boats of this size, the cable need only be 15 fathoms long. This is very little; the depth of water in an anchorage does not vary to suit the length of the boat using it, and if it is ten fathoms (a perfectly usual depth for an open anchorage) it is going to be a little difficult to apply the normal rules for calculating the scope! (See page 110 for the scope that should be allowed according to depth.)

In my opinion, a cable should never be shorter than forty fathoms, and it is reasonable to increase this figure to fifty to have some reserve when facing up to really bad conditions.

I have often had to anchor in depths of fifteen and even twenty fathoms off steep-to coasts, sometimes voluntarily, because the site provided good shelter, but on other occasions of necessity, for instance because rudder failure on the boat on which I was sailing left us at risk of being forced ashore. This sort of accident often happens as a result of the strain thrown on a boat's gear during a sudden squall, which was the case on that occasion. Without the anchor, stowed ready to let go on the stemhead and attached to its 45 fathom cable, the rocks to leeward of us might have been seriously damaged by our assault. . . .

Do not think I am making too much of this point. Remember, although the occasions on which you need an anchor to be in instant readiness are not very numerous, if it is not, then even the first time will be one too many.

Mixed cables The length of chain on a mixed cable should be roughly the length of the boat up to thirty feet: for larger boats it can be a little less, by perhaps 10 or 20%. This is as long as it is used only as a secondary cable; for a main anchor, French regulations impose a length of at least twice that of the boat for vessels over 9 metres. They are more optimistic than I am: as I have already said, I recommend an all-chain cable for the main anchor in all cases, for reasons of safety.

The warp should make up the total length to the figure given above: forty to fifty fathoms. There are two important points to cover in the making up of a mixed cable: the characteristics of each the components, and the strength and security with which they joined together.

Dimensions of anchor cables

Since 1980, French yachtsmen had to give up merely using own judgement (or that of favourite author) in deciding weight of chain or cable to use, the weight of the anchor, in favour of regulation requirements posed by law. These tables been retained in the English translation, as they are the result detailed and sensible research, I therefore regard the figures valuable guide to yachtsmen where in the world, although diameters given for the warp of a mixed cable are probably necessarily heavy.

French Regulation Weights For Anchors and Cables

Length (feet)	Deadweight (tonnes)	Weight of anchor (lb)	Diameter of chain (in)	(mm)	Diameter of warp (in)	(mm)
Up to 21	Up to 1	17½	¼	6	7/16	10
22–25	1–2	22	5/16	8	9/16	14
26–30	2–3	26½	5/16	8	9/16	14
31–34	3–4½	31	5/16	8	9/16	14
35–41	4½–8	35	3/8	9.5	¾	18
42–52	8–12	44	3/8	9.5	¾	18
53–59	12–16	53	7/16	12	11/12	22
60–65	16–20	75	7/16	12	11/12	22
66–82	20–30	88	9/16	14	1	24
–	25–30	132	5/8	16	1 15/16	28

Notes:
(1) Anchor weights in lb are converted from the metric figures: admittedly it may be difficult to find a 26½ lb anchor in countries using Imperial measure. It is interesting that the old English rule of thumb: 'A pound of anchor for each foot of boat' conforms very well with this table.
(2) The regulations provide that weights should be increased by one third if Fisherman or heavy-crowned Danforth types are used.
(3) Warps should be of 3-strand nylon, or have similar characteristics.
(4) If tonnage and length do not correspond in the table, the heavier gear is indicated.

Strength and Weight of Commonly used Rope

Diameter		Polypropylene		Terylene		Nylon	
(in)	(mm)	Breaking Strain (lb)	Weight/ Fathom (lb)	B/S (lb)	Weight/ Fathom (lb)	B/S (lb)	Weight Fathom (lb)
3/8	9	3080	0.2	3200	0.3	3750	0.
7/16	10	3650	0.25	4600	0.4	5500	0.
9/16	14	5070	0.35	6600	0.55	7500	0.
5/8	16	6400	0.45	8600	0.75	9500	0.
3/4	18	8400	0.5	10800	0.8	11700	0.
13/16	20	10150	0.65	13000	1.15	14800	0.
11/12	22	12100	0.75			18300	1.
1	24	14300	0.9			22050	1.

Strength and Weight of Anchor Chains

Diameter		Working Load (lb)	Breaking Strain (lb)	Weight (lb/fathom)
(in)	(mm)			
3/16	5	1100	2200	2.4
1/4	6.3	2200	4400	3.6
9/32	7	3300	6600	4.6
5/16	8	4400	8800	5.8
3/8	9.5	6600	13200	9.4
7/16	11.1	9900	14850	12.7

Length of Chain and Warp for Mixed Cables

(French official regulations)

Use	Boat (LOA feet)	Length of Chain	Length of W (fathoms
Main cable	Under 33	Twice boat length	25–30
Main cable	Over 33	Twice boat length	35–40
Secondary cable	Under 33	1½ × boat length	30–35
Secondary cable	Over 33	1½ × boat length	40–45

How to join the chain to the cable.
From top to bottom: (1) Loop in the chain made with shackle (pin secure with stainless steel wire); rope secured by round turn and bowline. (2) Th end of the knot is securely seized to the standing part. (3) The same chain loop passes through an eye splice with thimble. (4) If the gauge of the cha allows the shackle-pin to pass through, the shackle can be used to join the eye directly to the end link. (5) In emergency, the splice can be replaced b bowline, but please not insulating tape instead of seizing: not even for a photo!

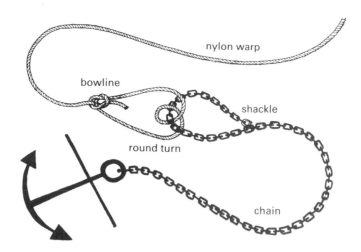

*re are several ways of joining the
~ponents of an anchor cable, but
~chever is adopted, it is vital to
~re the free ends of knots and the
~ of shackles, and to remember that
~ot reduces the strength of a rope
~t least a quarter.*

Joining warp to chain

~ strongest chain is no stronger
~ its weakest link. This old ad-
~ derives from pitiless logic, and
~inds us of the necessity to en-
~ the quality of any knots, shack-
~ or other devices used to join the
~erent components of an anchor
~le.

~t: only used on mixed cables,
~oin the chain to the warp. A
~erman's bend can be used, tied
~ctly through a shackle (see
~ch) or through a loop made in

~ast few links of the chain (see
~e). In either case the free end
~e knot must be firmly secured
~e standing part with Terylene
~ron) marline, even if, through
~ of time or knowledge, a bow-
~is used for this purpose. It is a
~ that the constant tightening
~slackening to which a cable is

subjected always tends to loosen a knot, particularly with the rather springy stranded ropes normally used for this job.

It must also be remembered that the presence of a knot reduces the strength of a rope by about 25%, whatever sort it is.

Shackle: normally only one in an all-chain cable, two in a mixed one. Care must be taken to tighten the pin firmly with pliers, and then secure it with stainless steel wire. This is vital. Obviously the diameter of the shackle should match that of the chain: 30% thicker section if it is a galvanised iron shackle, at least the same if it is stainless steel (this is better, because there is no risk of corrosion). Weakening the cable by using thinner shackles nullifies the advantage of having chosen stronger chain (1).

Chain-joining shackle: this is a shackle of identical calibre to the chain it is intended to join. Its advantage over the normal shackle is that once it is closed, it has no external difference from the other links of the chain, and will run easily over the bow roller or through a gipsy (2).

Bitter end: this is the name given to the end of the chain or cable furthest from the anchor. It should be attached to an eye bolt or other solid fixture attached to the main structure of the boat. Not with a shackle or iron wire, but with a cord gasket lashed with several turns

and easily accessible, so that it can easily be cut with a ship's knife if an emergency departure is needed. Because if one unhappy day you find reefs snarling under your stern, don't waste time trying to recover the anchor that has dragged: cut it adrift and escape from the trap!

Fisherman's bend
(1) The word shackle has another meaning. Chain is manufactured in relatively short lengths also called shackles, normally 30 fathoms or 60 metres. A shackle (or chain-joining shackle) may well be used, therefore, to join two shackles of chain.
(2) It is worth noting that chain made in one country will often not fit into a gipsy made in another, so if a replacement is needed while abroad, it is important to experiment before making an expensive and perhaps useless purchase.

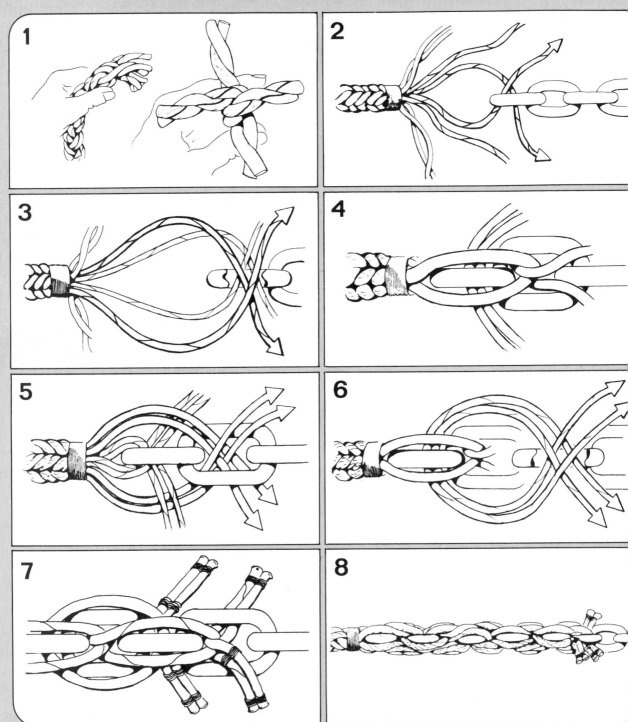

nlay the four main strands for a
equivalent to 12 links of the
, then put on a tight whipping to
t unlaying any further. Keep the
ds apart, one pair up, one down
he other two sideways. Start the
veaving with the horizontal ones.
elp identification, keep the ones
black threads as one pair, and
without as the other.

3) Take one black-threaded pair,
ate the two strands and pass them
through the first link. Then pass
cond pair (also black-threaded)
rough the same link. The two
ds from above should alternate
the two from below (see right-
part of Fig. 3).

art on the second link using the
ther pairs (without black thread)
e same way, passing the two
ds of each pair along the side of
st link on opposite sides before
ding through. The other pair will
readed through from the other
f this second link. Pull hard on
e strands. Make the third pass in
cal manner, returning to the four
ds with black threads.

6) Make the third pass in the third
with the two black-thread pairs,
ourth in the fourth link with the
ther pairs, and so on until the
ds have been passed through ten
five for each pair.

nish by seizing each pair together
se as possible to the links. Heat-
he ends for additional security.

he finished splice.
1 Marlow's Guide to Knots and
es.)

Securing the
secondary cable

The warp of the secondary cable
should also be firmly attached at
the bitter end. I remember being
awakened one night in a creek at
Piana, near Calvi in Corsica, by one
of Marc Linski's sailing-school
yachts, which had been anchored
not far from us on two anchors.
Tired of the swell which was penet-
rating the open bay where we had
taken refuge from a blow caused by
the winter *mistral*, its crew had
decided to set sail in the middle of
the night. 'Hey, you in the bows'
yelled the teacher-skipper, 'let out
the nylon warp as far as possible
while you get in the main anchor.
Go on! Pay out all the rest of it. . . .'
Then, a little later, 'Good, now the
main anchor is stowed, haul in the
other warp.' 'What warp?' replied a
shadow from the bows. 'You told
us to let it all out. . . .'

*This method of veering anchor chain
is definitely to be discouraged. First,
because boots should always be worn
when working on the foredeck,
secondly because a chain should never
be let out merely by hand, it should be
controlled by a turn round a samson
post or cleat. Especially on a boat of
this sort of tonnage.*

With a depth of twenty-five
metres (about thirteen fathoms), it
was no use diving. Especially in the
middle of the night, in February. If
you are interested, take a trip there
some day: you should still be able
to find it – a 45 lb CQR and fifty
fathoms of nylon warp. . . .

How do you avoid this sort of
accident? Don't forget to secure the
end of the warp. It doesn't matter
where, just somewhere strong
enough so that it won't be pulled
off while the crew are working on it.
You can't be too careful!

Part of Pitcairn's *anchorage arsenal.*
Grapnel, two tripping-line buoys, a
mooring buoy, a Fob-HP, a Britany
two CQRs (the one you can't see is
over the bow), 150 fathoms of 20 mr
warp, and enough different chains to
make anyone's head spin. . . .

Secondary ground-tack

I do not personally agree with
official (French) regulations, w
only require one anchor line o
boat under 30 ft. A second an
and cable is only obligatory
larger boats. While being stro
against all forms of regimenta
where cruising is concernee
sport which I would like to
protected from the bureaucrac
which our society is so prone),
worried by the sheer inadequae
these recommendations. Bec
instead of regarding them as a
minimum to be suppleme
according to circumstances, n
beginners may regard them as
finitive advice on the proper ec
ment to carry.

To set off in a 28 ft boat with
one anchor seems to me abou
sensible as crossing the Sa
with only one jerrycan of w
The risks of losing an anchor,
meeting conditions which ma
necessary to lie to two or
three during a strong squall, a
as much to small as to large b
from the moment they leave
bour and take to the open sea
second anchor may be use
provide a fork moor, or to ba
the main anchor (see page 1
seq.). To suppose that other
might come to their assistan
illusory, as well as being u
manlike. Anchorage crises us

CHARACTERISTICS OF THREE-STRAND ROPES IN METRIC MEASURES

Polyester (Terylene, Dacron)		
Diameter (mm)	Weight (g/m)	Breaking strain (kg)
5 mm	15 g	295 kg
6 mm	20 g	400 kg
8 mm	40 g	770 kg
10 mm	66 g	1270 kg
12 mm	97 g	1910 kg
15 mm	157 g	3180 kg
18 mm	205 g	4060 kg
20 mm	260 g	5080 kg
22 mm	320 g	6350 kg
24 mm	384 g	7620 kg

Polyamide (Nylon, Antron)		
5 mm	11 g	320 kg
6 mm	16 g	500 kg
8 mm	32 g	1020 kg
10 mm	53 g	1700 kg
12 mm	80 g	2500 kg
15 mm	128 g	4100 kg
18 mm	166 g	5300 kg
20 mm	210 g	6700 kg
22 mm	260 g	8300 kg
24 mm	315 g	10000 kg

Polypropylene (Nestron, Herculon)		
7 mm	17 g	550 kg
9 mm	30 g	960 kg
11 mm	45 g	1425 kg
13 mm	65 g	2030 kg
15 mm	90 g	2800 kg
18 mm	115 g	3500 kg
20 mm	148 g	4450 kg
22 mm	180 g	5370 kg
24 mm	220 g	6500 kg
26 mm	260 g	7600 kg

up suddenly, and if the situa-
is saved it is often by action
in the few subsequent
nds.

ave never dallied in the Magel-
Straits or suffered the caresses
Indonesian typhoon; even so,
e lost count of the occasions
an emergency has forced me
rab *Pitcairn*'s number three
or from its stowage. As for the
to use two anchors in an open
orage, at night or in rising
, that seems to me to be
us. We will talk more of that

t to be going on with, one
ld accept that a cruising yacht
ot safely put to sea without the
wing equipment:

Main or Bower anchor: an anchor and an all-chain cable, 40 fathoms long for boats under 33 ft, 50 for those over.

Secondary anchors (Kedges): an anchor with a mixed cable of the same length as the main cable, and a third anchor and cable if the boat is over 33 feet.

On long-distance cruises, a fourth anchor will prove useful in case of going aground, and circum-navigating authors make it clear that this is no rare occurrence. Moitessier, Erling Tambs, Bardiaux, Alain Gerbault, Jean Lacombe, Van God and many others have de-scribed this in some detail. So carry an extra anchor and sleep better!

The Teddy *was an old pilot cutter, which had spent years cruising the dangerous reef-strewn shores of Norway before being lost one day in the southern summer, at the other side of the world from her native town of Larvik.*

Erling Tambs, a Norwegian novelist whose character was as tough as his Colin Archer boat (built, like Nansen's famous *Fram*, in his home town of Larvik), was an extraordinary person. Although his abilities as a sailor fell far short of his qualities as a man, he has left us a remarkable book, full of simplicity, in which every line reflects the spirit of a happy-go-lucky adventurer, quite unlike any marine author writing today. If it is their very weaknesses that make some people likeable, the epic he recounts here serves only to add another mistake to the score of this maladroit hero. A fatal mistake, because the fact that his anchor was not stowed at the ready cost him what he loved most in all the world after his family: the *Teddy*, in which he had already sailed half-way round the world by this 9th March 1930.

'I had decided to moor alongside the little jetty at Mansion House Bay (on Kawau, a little island in New Zealand, 30 miles from Auckland) to avoid the bother and sweat of anchoring, as the anchor was firmly lashed in place in the forepeak, while its chain was stowed right aft in the little stern-cabin. . . . Waking the next morning, we found that the easterly breeze had changed to a strong gale from the northeast. . . .

'In the entrance to the bay, we unfortunately found only a light southerly breeze, not enough to enable us to make headway against the strong northgoing tidal stream. *Even so, after several hours of tacking we managed to weather the reefs: from there, it was a broad reach for the southern point of Challenger Island, a rocky islet hardly four hundred yards long from north to south, and divided by a narrow channel from the southeast point of Kawau.*

'The gale had left behind it a heavy swell, which broke with a sound like thunder on the rocks of the point. As we approached, the breeze seemed to strengthen a little, but the current carried us swiftly to leeward, and by the time we were a hundred yards off, it became clear that we would not weather them. By then the point was east of us, and the Teddy *was making southeast.*

'Consequently, I put the tiller down to go about. To my intense surprise, the boat refused to answer. . . . I tried again, trying the effect of jerking the tiller sharply downwind again and again: nothing! I was filled with consternation.

'We were being carried faster and faster onto the rocks, where the swell was hurling itself in gigantic breakers which, crashing onto the rocks, burst roaring into cataracts of spray. Thirty, twenty yards away the sunken rocks seemed to be gnashing their teeth. The noise was deafening. . . . We felt ourselves caught by an undertow that gave off a smell of mould and decay. I was in despair: the end of the Teddy *was near.*

'We struck. I felt the keel smash itself on the rocks. The Teddy *wallowed,* then picked herself up, was c[...] again by a wave and hurled forw[...] right into the breakers. I scream[...] my wife to get little Tui who was [...] down in the cabin. At that mome[...] enormous wave picked up the T[...] and hurled her beam-on onto [...] rocks.*

'Everything happened at [...] Planks were smashed, spars went f[...] with cracks like thunder. The[...] screamed, roared and leaped wit[...] noise of ten thousand unchaine[...] mons of the deep. . . . Pitilessly, [...] tide fell, the undertow dragge[...] unhappy victim from the cliff, h[...] her smashed timbers against the pr[...] tions from the rocky bottom, shatt[...] and tearing and finally abande[...] her, heeling far over, half the [...] smothered in foam while the b[...] continued to lash furiously an[...] spume-covered whirlpools which [...] rounded it. Then a wave would a[...] lift and throw the heavy hulk [...] again onto the boulders. I think I [...] never suffered so much. . . .'

(From *Honeymoon in the St[...]* the excellent account by E[...] Tambs, French edition by A[...] Dumont, 1952.)

Above, a chart of New Zealand, w[...] the Teddy *was wrecked. Left, Erli[...] Tambs, photographed aboard wit[...] dog, Emergency Rations.*

Above, a chart of New Zealand, where the Teddy *was wrecked. Left, Erling Tambs, photographed aboard with his dog,* Emergency Rations.

41

STOWAGE OF ANCHORING GEAR

Because of their cumbrousness, and also their weight, anchors and their gear always present a stowage problem, above all when there are several aboard. It is therefore quite common to see a skipper diving into a stern locker or rummaging under a crew member's bunk to produce the anchor needed for a Sunday picnic in an open anchorage. Indeed, it's a bit of luck if, in the rush, he doesn't have to use the mainsheet for a cable because he can't lay his hands on the proper one.

Don't smile: this sort of exhibition can be seen more often than you might think, and not just on motor cruisers or chartered yachts, either. I remember going aboard for a 24-hour passage not so long ago, and we had got right across to the other side of the Channel before the owner of the boat succeeded in tracking down the one and only anchor warp aboard. . . .

VITAL RULES:

● **The main anchor** on a coastal cruise should always be in the bows, within reach of a man on deck, and completely equipped. Never separate the anchor from its chain or warp for whatever motive. If an error in navigation or a failure of gear happens close inshore one must be able to anchor instantaneously, which will only be possible if the main cable is ready for immediate use on the stemhead or close by.

● **The second anchor** should be permanently ready for use, and the different elements making it up should never be detached from each other. Anchor and cable should be stowed either on deck (aboard *Pitcairn* it is permanently lashed forward of the mainmast, and it is often used), or in a locker preferably near the bows: the sail locker or a purpose-built anchor well are suitable. It is essential to be able to bring it into use quickly, in case the main chain refuses to pay out through the chain-hawse (this

has been known to happen in so hulls as a result of deformation to heavy seas), or when accidental grounding necessita the rapid use of two anchors.

● **The other auxiliary anch** should if possible be stowed a times shackled to their length chain. One should get into the h of considering anchor and chai an inseparable unity, one be quite useless without the other they should be made up once for all. Would you stow eyepiece and the frame of y sextant in two different lockers practice it is always possible to somewhere where they can stowed without being separa The position will be chosen bea good distribution of weight mind. For these auxiliary anch called into use only exceptiona the bottom of a locker or a sp below the sole will do, as long this stowage is clearly inventor As for the warps to complete set, these can be stowed in a d locker or beneath the sole, but m be easily accessible in any ever

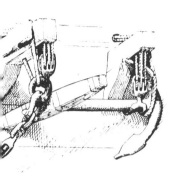

secondary anchor at the foot of
mast. Below: galvanised iron
[shac]kles cannot be unscrewed once
[they] have spent some time in salt
[wate]r. Hurrah for stainless steel, much
[more] helpful! Even after ten years.

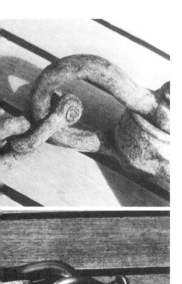

Chain lockers

Built into the extreme fore-part of the bow and vertically below the chain-pipe on deck, this independant compartment resolves the problem of the stowage of the main anchor chain in a convenient manner.

Advantages:
• providing a volume of stowage with no direct communication with the rest of the boat, which allows direct drainage of the large amount of water that runs from the chain as it is raised. The living quarters are protected from the damp (and sometimes smells) which result.
• being situated in the extreme bow, thus close to the anchor winch
• allowing the stowage of the chain by its own weight as it falls from the gipsy, or from hand as hauled in
• leaving the foredeck unencumbered during anchoring and weighing.

Possible Disadvantages:
• isolation of the chain leading to lack of maintenance
• access hatch sometimes difficult to get at (under a forecabin bunk or the sail-locker sole)
• position causing the presence of a substantial weight at the extreme forward part of the boat which can, in certain hulls, cause excessive pitching

• frequent formation of tangles in the chain after heavy weather, preventing it from paying out freely through the chain pipe
• piling of the chain into a pyramid which can mean that, even though there is plenty of room in the locker, the mouth of the chain pipe becomes blocked before the whole length is stowed.

Recommendations:
Whether the boat is metal, wooden or plastic, the locker should be double lined, because the repeated battering from chain sliding about in a heavy sea can cause severe deterioration. That is to say nothing of the possibility of erosion or electrolysis which may occur in metal hulls.

As far as possible the bottom of the chain locker should be cut off from the rest of the interior of the boat, and provided with a drain hole designed to facilitate the passage of weed back into the sea. It is imperative that its access hatch be easy to get at, to allow regular examination of the contents, the disentangling of knots in the chain, or even the cutting of the lashing securing the bitter end in case the cable has to be slipped in a hurry.

The chain pipe (stainless steel for preference) should be stopped against heavy seas by a rag plug or a special cap. The pipe, which should widen out below the deck, should not be too long, to avoid

blockages caused by the chain piling up underneath it. One last point: if your boat has a winch, make sure that the chain pipe is vertically below the after side of the gipsy, so that the chain falls straight down into the locker — without loitering on the way!

The anchor well

As long as its method of opening is both robust and well thought out, an anchor-well built into the plan of the foredeck can provide an excellent solution to the stowage problem. It can be used either to contain the whole of the secondary gear (both anchor and mixed cable), or just the mixed cable for the main anchor for those who insist on that option, the anchor being secured on the stemhead. In this latter case the chain locker loses its use, except perhaps for the stowage of an emergency chain.

Main points to watch
● the drainage holes which, with the chain locker, should b sufficient diameter to allow v and sand brought up by the c to escape
● the solidity of the hinges of hatch cover and its retaining port when open (remember it r be able to stand up to a good l life on the foredeck is someti rather a scramble)
● the presence of an effec catch (preferably one whose lease does not stand proud): vital that the anchor cable s securely retained in heavy wea
● the dimensions of the v which must be adequate for chosen anchor (not necessarily that folds flat) and, if there is chain locker, for an adequate le of cable
● the presence of fixing point hold the cable while in use, an the case of an all-chain cabl solid strong point for the bitter of the chain.

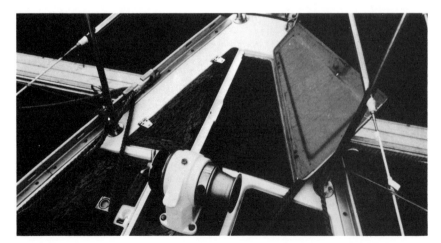

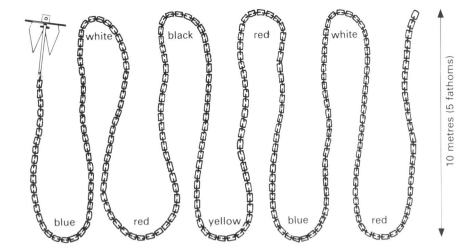

ain chain in glorious Technicolor
w, what a job!). For my part I use
French and Belgian flags as a
monic for the stripes of colour
ted on my anchor chains: I just
e to remember the order of the
urs on the flags. The marks are
ted on every ten metres (five
oms).

white   black   red   white

blue   red   yellow   blue   red

10 metres (5 fathoms)

rking anchor cables

en preparing to anchor, every-
e knows (and we will discuss the
tter at some length in a later
pter) that the length of im-
rsed cable, that is, the scope,
es as a function of a number of
ameters, among them the depth
water and the strength of the
d. Knowing how to calculate
t ten fathoms of chain are
ded is one thing: measuring out
t chain with sufficient accuracy
quite another. I always wonder
w crews manage aboard boats
ose cables are unmarked. 'Veer
fathoms' announces the skip-
, shoving the main boom up-
d to make the boat gather stern-
y. 'Ten fathoms gone', replies
crewman on the foredeck a few
onds later. Just like that, with-
measuring or special marks,
t by watching the Atlantic run-
g along the side of the hull. . . .
was at lle d'Yeu in the Anse des
rbeaux. The wind proving a little
co-operative, the skipper cor-
ted after a moment: 'Another
e fathoms, that will be safer. . . .'
good period of clanking from
windlass, followed suddenly
an uppercut that made the
ole boat vibrate right up to the
sthead. 'There's no more chain'
laimed the foredeck hand,
e're on the bitter end!' 'No more
ain? You're joking: that cable's
fathoms long. . . .' And the crew

retorted, shrugging his shoulders,
'You ought to have marked the
damn thing, old fruit. I tell you,
we've let out the whole lot'.

To avoid all hesitation or any
arguments, mark your chains. Every five fathoms, paint a coloured
band about a foot long. Myself, I
use successively the colours of the
French and Belgian flags: a blue
band, a white, a red, then a black, a
yellow and a red . . . and start again
until we get to the bitter end. It is
infallible: when the white band
reaches the stemhead, ten fathoms
are over. If it is the yellow, that
means twenty-five, if the black,
twenty. As for red, experience
shows that there is rarely any doubt
between 15, 30 or 45 fathoms,
especially if the 30 is marked by a
double band and the 45 by a triple

one.

Warp is marked in the same way,
but by means of strips of cloth
slipped in between the strands of
the rope and sewn into place. Strips
of spinnaker nylon are perfect for
the job, the ideal length being about four inches. By this method,
main and secondary cables are
marked in exactly the same way.
What could be easier!

This mnemonic system has the
advantage of needing no code of
reference. As long, of course, as
everyone knows the order of the
stripes on the flags! Readers in
other countries will of course be
able to devise their own equivalents: three colours are ample if the
system of double and triple bands
is used, as for example red, white,
blue, red red, white white etc.

ıs aboard Nausicaa, *my previous*
ı, that some memorable blasts
ı the meltemi *in the Aegean taught*
ı lot about anchoring.

Anchor Trials

nd suddenly began to come in from
great Atlantic swell. I hurriedly cut
t my walk and embarked in my
n. Carola's stern chains, snubbing
gerously high out of the water,
ped. I was able to cast off my bow
ɔs, but the boats started off on a
dance! Several times the little cutter
carried right under Carola's *coun-*
horrible sight! I just avoided being
shed. Kurun's *mast sent the*
ɔner's ensign-staff flying. The
ı hanging chains wound themselves
ıd my boom. I just managed to
ıtangle them before any damage
done, and succeeded in casting off
warps that held the cutter at the
ı. Taking advantage of a brief lull,
ɔpped my anchor, but it dragged.
ıtle way away, the harbour bottom
appearing and disappearing again:
ɾrifying sight. If the cutter had
ɾged that far, she would have been
shed to pieces.'

ɔm Kurun Round the World *by J-Y*
Toumelin, Flammarion.)

his incident took place in Febru-
1950 in the port of Casablanca,
rocco, as a result of a severe
ter gale. Jacques-Yves Le
ımelin succeeded, not without
iculty, in getting an anchor to
d before his cutter was smashed
the bottom of the basin. This
ry illustrates how vital it is to be
ɛ to count on the holding power
the anchors one carries: when
y drag, the consequences are
often dramatic simply because it
always happens in bad weather.

As far as I know, Le Toumelin
always used Fisherman anchors.
Since the time when he sailed
round the world, considerable advances have been made in anchors
and associated gear. Not only
through the improved strength of
chain and warps, but also on the
one hand through the greater
acceptance of the CQR on pleasure
craft, and on the other, through the
development of new designs (Danforth, etc), the reliability of modern
anchors has undoubtedly brought a
great improvement in safety standards in yachting. Ten years ago
and more, I remember dragging
often in open anchorages, even in
light breezes and with little current,
using gear which, although unsuit-
able, was yet widely used on
yachts. The improvement was due
to the research of the inventors,
and to the experience acquired by
the increasing number of users.
Information was circulated by articles and by word of mouth, and a
selection of reliable models gradually came to the fore. A selection
which was, however, tested by various organisations, who all arrived
at different evaluations, which
often proved to be contradictory,
thus perplexing the readers of the
varying accounts.

So let us return to the question
posed in the first chapter, when we
studied various models of anchor.
How can one make a comparative
test of anchors, and what confidence can be placed in it?

Can an anchor be tested?

The report by the National Sailing
School of Beg-Rohu, based on tests
carried out in the autumn of 1980
(which we will look at carefully on
pages 51–62), begins with the following caution:
'Generalisations from these results
should be strictly avoided: they are
only valid in the experimental condi-
tions described. Other tests will be
needed to study the influence of other
factors which might intervene and
modify the results recorded.'

This warning does credit to the
organisation responsible, and
should be borne in mind by the
various manufacturers concerned.
In fact, conclusions drawn from
comparative trials on anchors are
only valid within the limits imposed
by the control methods decided
upon by the organisers of the various tests. For the rest, the
methods used vary very little from
one test to another: trials are
generally carried out beside a
beach with the aid of a fixed winch
or a mobile tractor, or on an area of
calm water using a motor boat. For
reasons of convenience and lack of
choice, the bottom is most usually

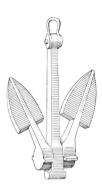

sand or gravel, rarely rock or weed. Also, the pull exerted on the cable is invariably along a constant line of traction, and at a constant force.

These are parameters which tend, by their specialisation, if not to falsify the value of the results, at least to produce information from which it would be dangerous to make generalisations.

Reliability of the results

One must bear in mind that in real life, the forces acting on an anchor are singularly different. In an open anchorage, for instance, the cable will suffer changes in direction due to the pressures of squalls, and through variations in the direction of the wind or, in tidal waters, stream. These changes in the direction of pull produce mechanical effects on the working surface of the anchor, perhaps resulting in its breaking out through unbalancing or pivoting. (How, in these tests, could one ever study the accidents of fouling of the anchor, so often a cause of disaster in the anchorages of grandfather's day?) Again, the heavy shocks due to snubbing under the assault of wind or swell have considerable effect on the holding of an anchor. Indeed, it is the simultaneous occurrence of these two elements, change in the direction of pull and violent snubbing, that most often breaks out an anchor.

48

...wo adjacent photographs, taken ...Y. Leroux during the trials at ...Rohu, show the methods used in ...or trials. Left, a 25 hp tractor. ...t, the boat used for underwater ...on the different models. As for the ...haired siren, watching alone from ...erch on the pulpit, the report ...es no mention of her. . . .

...sting my mind back to a three-...k stay in the Caribbean, mainly ...t in open anchorages with ...ds of exceptional muscle, I am ...again reminded of the effects ...luced by the combination of ...e two forces. They act with ...rising brutality. To discover the ...tions of a particular anchor ...ssitates prolonged experi-...itation in real-life conditions ...varying circumstances. For a ...parative test to attain similar ...lts, the organisers would have ...e able to reproduce all possible ...ditions of use, quite impossible ...imulate artificially at moderate

...iis inability to bring together ...parameters needed for a com-...e control obliges the testers to ...e a choice. We still have to find ...how this choice is made, and by ...t criteria it is governed. To ...ver this question one essential ...t has first to be raised: who ...inises these tests, and why?

Who organises the tests?

...will only discuss serious tests, ...ed out by experienced bodies ...ible of imposing precise con-...-. These tests are made at the ...est of an inventor or manufac-...r, with a view to discovering the ...ities of an existing design or of

a new prototype. An international bureau of control may be entrusted with making the actual tests; but even then the results remain the property of the 'client', that is the person or company who has financed the operation. When questioned on this subject, the management of the *Bureau Véritas*, whose strict standards have earned it a high reputation, confirmed to me that its findings came under the heading of professional secrets, and only the initiator of the investigation had the right to divulge them. Or to keep them quiet.

So how are these things really arranged?

Without wishing to throw the least doubt on the honesty and good faith of the researchers concerned, whom I know to be both competent and rigorous technicians, it is still a fact that their inventions, in order to achieve wide sales, have to be commercialised. And prove their efficacy. If you produce a tyre that gives exceptional performance on dry roads, you do not choose a wet day to carry out tests intended to be published. Especially comparative ones. . . . It is precisely this orientation of the test conditions that explains the diversity of the results observed. It is thus only necessary for a producer to undergo a test of this type, for his product, as if by a miracle, to come out top of the list. There is no

other result possible: if it doesn't, he will not publish the results.

I need no more for proof of this than the papers put out by the firms of Plastimo, and Britany Forgings and Laminations, the two main French anchor makers. The tests organised by these two firms are a revelation: at Beg-Rohu, the Britany MK-2 pulverised all records in holding power, whereas at St-Brieuc the Fob-HP was crowned champion in all categories. As I have already made clear, the tests in both cases were conducted with

the greatest care for honesty and exactitude. It is just that the conditions chosen proved to be more favourable for one model or the other. Which, after all, is not difficult to understand, as both anchors possess individual qualities of real value.

And we have our own knowledge, we who, outside the laboratory, test them of necessity when wind and sea attack us in our

anchorages. We know that on firm sand the Fisherman anchor is slow to take hold, but that it is marvellous in weed. We know that a CQR will not drag when the tide turns off l'Aberwrac'h. We know that the Danforth, thanks to its stock, will bury itself in the sand without breaking out if the chain snubs hard. We know that the Britany and the Fob-HP are effective as long as they are not broken out as a result of swinging. We know these things from experience, just as from sailing the seas in bad weather one finally learns what sails are best for one's boat on such a heading and in such a sea.

Until an independent organisation, constrained by no financial interest, can test anchors under the real conditions of use, we will only read limited reports on the behaviour of these capricious instruments. Indications only, from which we must guard against drawing too hasty conclusions or making too wide-ranging generalisations.

This is by no means to suggest that these studies are worthless. On the contrary, a scrutiny of them provides a series of exact observations, no less concrete for being limited in scope. The series of tests at Beg-Rohu, in taking the case of a boat moored bow to quay over a bottom of submerged (and therefore firm) sand, provided highly useful comparisons for this particular situation. And that is how they should be used.

Conducted by people of experience and widely reported in the press, this series of tests is interesting on more than one count. It shows in particular the extent to which the publication of exact figures, without detailed explanation, can produce misleading information, even in the pages of specialist magazines.

Marine anchor foundry, engraving Robert Bénard from Diderot's Encyclopédie *(Vol.* **III**, *1769). An where electronics has scarcely had a effect on modern techniques. Two centuries later, anchor manufacture still craftsmen's work.*

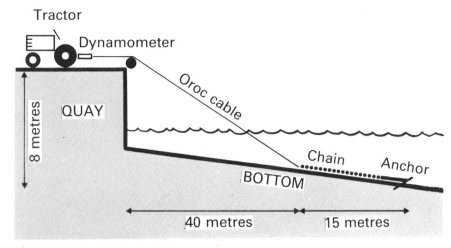

Tractor
Dynamometer
Oroc cable
QUAY
8 metres
Chain
Anchor
BOTTOM
40 metres
15 metres

Anatomy of a trial

28th October 1980, Alain Con-
, head of the research depart-
it of the National Sailing School
eg-Rohu, organised a compara-
study of anchors at Quiberon,
e request of inventor Armand
n and the Plastimo company.
Brocheton of *Bureau Véritas*
charged with the official con-
of the experiments. (The major-
of the facts enumerated in this
were drawn from the report
le by M. Connan.)

Anchors tested:

en anchors in total, of which
Bruces were so much heavier
n the other models (20 kg −
), that we were unable to take
n into account, and a Sea Grip
ch could not be tested in the
n part of the test (submerged)
technical reasons. We therefore
in only the following eight
hors:

- Britany MK-1, 12 kilos (26½ lb)
- Britany MK-2, 12 kilos (with folding stabilisers)
- Light Alloy Britany, 7 kilos (15½ lb) (with folding stabi- lisers)
- Bruce, 10 kilos (22 lb)
- CQR, 11.3 kilos (25 lb)
- Fob-HP, 12 kilos
- Maria-Theresa, 12 kilos
- Salle, 12 kilos.

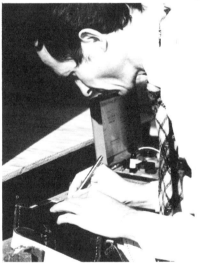

Sites Chosen:

The tests were conducted on two
different sites:

(1) **Preliminary controls out of the
water**: the sandy beach near the
Beg-Rohu school, in the part without rocks. Used at half-tide falling,
the wet sand was not totally free
from contained air.

(2) **Underwater tests**: also a sandy
bottom, near the outer part of the
school's jetty, with a depth of 1.7
metres (5½ ft) at low water. Thus, a
compact bottom, with no contained
air (see sketch).

Experimental Apparatus:

We will confine ourselves to mentioning the set-up for the underwater experiments, as the preliminary
test, with horizontal traction on an
uncovered beach, is too far removed from normal usage.

The equipment used comprised a
25 hp tractor pulling at a speed of
4–8 inches per second on a mixed
cable composed of an Oroc cable
and a 9.5 mm (⅜") chain shackled
to the anchor under test. The cable
was led to the back of the tractor
through a block of negligible resistance.

Measuring Instruments:

- a mechanical dynamometer
- a Vishay-Micromesures exten-
sometric chain reading from 0–
1000 kilos
- other equipment including standard weights and a portable
machine which allowed graphic records of the forces measured to be
produced on the spot.

The results given by the electronic measuring chain were checked
against the standard weights and
measures in each of the preliminary tests as a validity control. The
close correspondence of the two
sets of results allowed the measuring chain alone to be used in the
underwater tests.

RESULTS OF THE TESTS ON 8 ANCHORS CARRIED OUT ON 28TH OCTOBER 1980 AT BEG-ROHU (PART 1)

Presentation of the results

The resistance graphs which I have designed were created from the readings taken during the deep water tests. The vertical scale shows resistance measured in kilograms, the horizontal scale the horizontal displacement of the tractor in metres. The following figures can be derived from the graphs:

(1) Resistance force at its maximum level

(2) Resistance force at its lowest level after the previous reading

(3) Wave length: that is, in the case of the two cyclical anchors, Britany MK-1 and Fob-HP, the distance of displacement between the phases of breaking out and re-setting

(4) Resistance force over a metre, measured at one or other maximum for the two cyclical anchors, or in an area of constant resistance near the maximum for the six others.

The photos which accompany them were taken by J. Y. Leroux of the school, during the preliminary tests on uncovered sand. The examination of these results produces valuable information about the behaviour of each model. One notes particularly in number 3 the surprising power of the Britany MK-2, sadly still at the prototype stage a year after these tests.

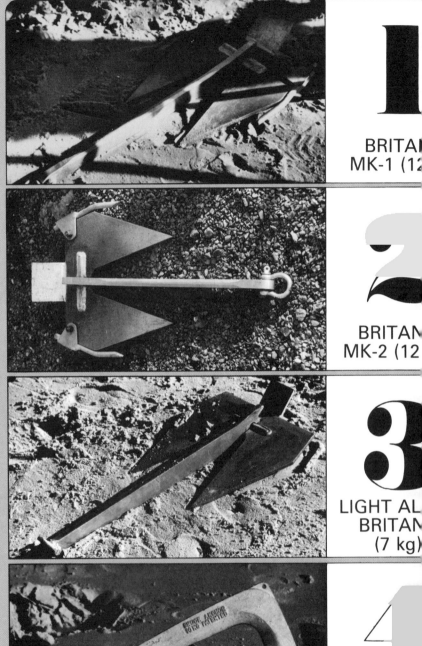

1 BRITANY MK-1 (12

2 BRITANY MK-2 (12

3 LIGHT ALLOY BRITANY (7 kg)

4 BRUCE (10 kg

52

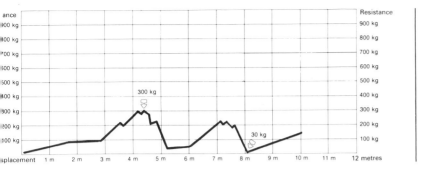

SUMMARY

Anchor model:
Britany MK-1 steel.
Weight: 12 kg
Resistance force:
maximum 300 kg,
minimum 30 kg.
Dragging distance 2.75 m
Resistance over 1 m: 222 kg.

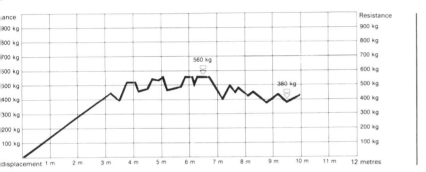

SUMMARY

Anchor model:
Britany MK-2 steel.
Weight: 12 kg.
Resistance force:
maximum 560 kg, minimum 380 kg.
Dragging distance negligible.
Resistance over 1 m: 527 kg.

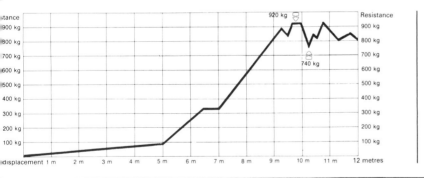

SUMMARY

Anchor model:
Britany MK-2 aluminium.
Weight: 7 kg.
Resistance force:
maximum 920 kg, minioum 740 kg.
Dragging distance negligible.
Resistance over 1 m: 855 kg.

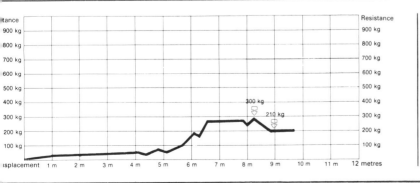

SUMMARY

Anchor model:
Bruce.
Weight: 10 kg.
Resistance force:
maximum 300, minimum 210 kg.
Dragging distance negligible.
Resistance over 1 m: 265 kg.

See conversion chart at end of book for equivalent imperial measures.

RESULTS OF THE TESTS ON 8 ANCHORS CARRIED OUT ON 28TH OCTOBER 1980 AT BEG-ROHU (PART 2)

5
CQR
(11.3 k

6
FOB-H
(12 kg

Detailed Analysis of the Results

Influence of shape: The phenomenon of the modification of density in the deposits making up the bottom, which increases with depth, partially explains the more elevated performances observed during these trials. Those anchors whose design encourages them to dig in well show, as a direct consequence, a higher resistance force for equivalent weight.

Influence of weight: This was of little importance in the experimental conditions of these trials. The light alloy Britany, with a greater surface than that of the MK-2 model for much less weight, gave the best results (let us remember that the alloy Britany reproduced the shape of the 16 kilo model for a weight of only 7 kilos, while the MK-2 in steel, of reduced dimensions, weighs 12 kilos). We should note for information that the 20 kilo Bruce produced a resistance over 1 metre of 330 kilos, while the 10 kilo model scored 265 kilos: a very small improvement for such a large difference in weight. It remains to be seen whether on a bottom of thick weed, the lighter weight may not risk reducing the chances of this anchor getting through to the bottom. It would need a more advanced experiment to tell us this.

7
MARIA
THERES
(12 kg)

8
SALLE
(12 kg)

54

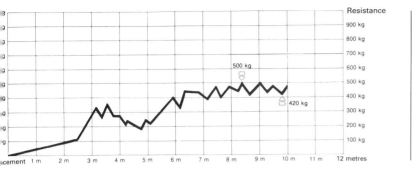

SUMMARY

Anchor model:
25 lb CQR.
Weight:
Resistance force:
maximum 500 kg, minimum 420 kg.
Dragging distance negligible.
Resistance over 1 m: 425 kg

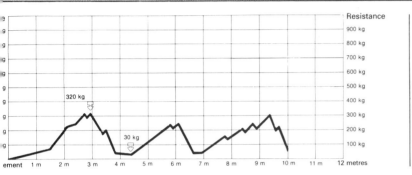

SUMMARY

Anchor model:
Fob-HP.
Weight: 12 kg.
Resistance force:
maximum 320 kg, minimum 30 kg.
Dragging distance: 2.60 m
Resistance over 1 m: 242 kg.

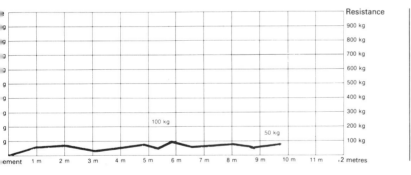

SUMMARY

Anchor model
Maria-Theresa.
Weight 12 kg.
Reistance force:
maximum 100 kg, minimum 50 kg.
Resistance over 1 m: 74 kg.

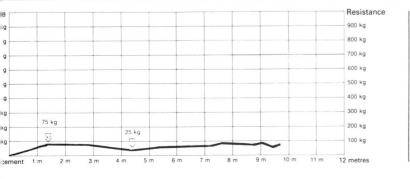

SUMMARY

Anchor model:
Salle.
Weight 12 kg.
Resistance force:
maximum 75 kg, minimum 25 kg.
Resistance over 1 m: 65 kg.

See conversion chart at end of book for equivalent imperial measures.

Preparation for a test in the presence of the inventor, the builder and the observer from Véritas.

Comparative Analysis

After initial study of the graphs produced, the organisers of the trials divided the anchors tested into three groups:

- **Anchors of low resistance** (Maria-Theresa and Salle)
- **cyclical anchors** (Britany MK-1 and Fob-HP)
- **anchors of high and continuous resistance** (Britany aluminium and MK-2, CQR and Bruce).

The report by the National Sailing School limits its analysis to the objects of the research, and acquits itself very well. But some additional comments are necessary to clarify the results.

1

Anchors of low resistance

Indisputably, there are grounds to distrust these models, at least as regards the chosen bottom. Their holding power hardly exceeds that derived purely from the weight of anchor and chain. This result confirms the poor chances their points have of digging in, probably caused by the wide, heavy crowns reminiscent of early Fob designs. In spite of the traction conditions, which were undoubtedly favourable to them, these anchors were shown by this test to be totally ineffectual. We shall see later that the St-Brieuc trials are more favourable to the Salle, without there being any obvious way of explaining the difference in the findings.

2

Cyclical anchors

This delicately chosen name scribes those anchors that br out under a certain traction for The results give some support those users who complained, fore the appearance of the Brita prototypes, that anchors based the Danforth concept tended drag suddenly, and thereafter fused to re-engage. This type breakout is seriously worry when one realises that in real us occurs as a result of a violent which tends to drive the boat ast with some speed. There is no do that this speed causes problems this type of anchor in getting a g of the bottom again. It is theref important to realise that the c

Results at Beg-Rohu on 28th October 1980

Model	Material	Weight of anchor	Resistance force max.	Resistance force min.	Dragging distance	Resistance over 1 metre
1 Britany MK-1	steel	12 kg	300 kg	30 kg	2·75m	222 kg
2 Britany MK-2	steel	12 kg	560 kg	380 kg	—	527 kg
3 Light alloy Britany	light alloy	7 kg	920 kg	740 kg	—	855 kg
4 Bruce	steel	10 kg	300 kg	210 kg	—	265 kg
5 CQR 25 lb	steel	11·3 kg	500 kg	420 kg	—	425 kg
6 Fob-HP	steel	12 kg	320 kg	30 kg	2·60m	242 kg
7 Maria-Theresa	steel	12 kg	100 kg	50 kg	—	74 kg
8 Salle	steel	12 kg	75 kg	25 kg	—	65 kg

⋯ed speed of the tractor un-⋯btedly favoured their re-⋯agement as observed in the ⋯s.

⋯ cause of this breaking out? The ⋯ing School's report describes at ⋯ a phase during which the ⋯hor digs in progressively, until it ⋯appears, completely buried; at ⋯ point the resistance increases ⋯ maximum value. Now it turns ⋯r onto its side and re-emerges ⋯n the soil a few metres further ⋯ before beginning to dig in ⋯in. When this cycle appears to ⋯regular, the measurement of the ⋯tances involved might seem to ⋯ a useful figure to retain in the ⋯ults. Unless you think about it. In ⋯ life, with the traction force ⋯reasing at the same time as the ⋯ed of movement over the bot-⋯n, it will soon reach such a ⋯mentum under the pressure of ⋯ wind that the chances of the ⋯hor re-engaging will virtually ⋯appear; by then, only a rock will ⋯ able to stop it in its tracks.

⋯hat is the danger with these ⋯clical' anchors, which are only ⋯ective up to the point where they ⋯ak out, and no further. The im-⋯rtant thing is therefore to know ⋯ limit of traction force which ⋯st not be exceeded. In measure-⋯nts with the pull in a constant ⋯ection, the trials put this suf-⋯ently high for a respectable mar-⋯ of safety to be preserved. In the ⋯t chapter we will examine the ⋯ces exercised on a sailing boat in ⋯ anchorage: they remain below ⋯s limit. To consider higher trac-⋯n forces than this does not have ⋯y significance as far as use on ⋯chts is concerned.

Anchors of high and continuous resistance

It will be noted that two distinct types of anchor can be classed under this heading:

● **Ploughshare anchors:** CQR and Bruce. These anchors demons-trated their power of constant re-sistance, whatever their weight. I was surprised by the Bruce, be-cause it has been claimed that on a sandy bottom its shape requires a preliminary burial of its blade, either by manual intervention or by leaving it time to imbed itself (as with the Fisherman types). The CQR remains for its part the most effective of the available models, confirming its reputation for high holding power. Note that its resist-ance to traction was remarkable under the test conditions.

● **Flat-bladed anchors:** The new generation Britany has lateral stabi-lisers. It is precisely the presence of these folding half-stocks that ex-plains the high holding power in sand of the improved Britany. What happens down there on the bot-tom? We have analysed the be-haviour of flat-bladed anchors with narrow crowns, typed as 'cyclical' at Beg-Rohu, which turn sideways after burying themselves and there-after break out under a pull with some elevation. The American Dan-forth, which is narrow crowned

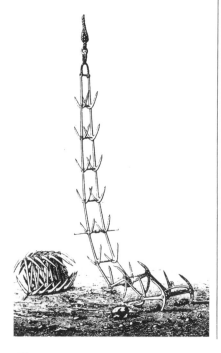

'The Renard anchor is a sort of ladder made of hooks weighing 45 kilos (100 lb) and measuring 5 metres (16 ft) in length. The cable, originally of hemp, is now steel, which allows its length to be increased to 500–1000 metres.'
Supplementary detail: invented in 1905, this monstrosity equipped . . . an airship!

with narrow flukes, does not suffer from this problem of breaking out. It penetrates into the sand more and more deeply under strain without turning sideways, thanks to its stock (in a comparative trial carried out at St-Brieuc, it became so deeply buried that it seems to have been impossible to recover it). The stabilisers on the new Britany offer the same advantage, without the encumbrance on deck. This makes one regret the absence of a Danforth from this trial, because it would have been interesting to compare the performance of anchors of the same type under these conditions. I myself have never used this American anchor, but having sailed a good deal in the Caribbean and also California, I am well aware how popular it is on that side of the Atlantic, where it shares the market with the CQR. I shall be off to the Virgin Islands in three weeks' time with *Pitcairn*, and I intend to equip myself with a 45 lb Danforth in order to complete my knowledge of the subject, by studying it in parallel with the three other models I have aboard.

FROM ONE TRIAL TO THE OTHER

A few months before, Brittany Forgings and Laminations had carried out a comparative trial of a similar kind, under the technical control of APAVE (1) at Binic in the Bay of St-Brieuc. We reproduce here the data provided by this controlled test:

Comparative trial of 12 kilo (25 lb) anchor

- Carried out on 22nd August on the motor-launch *Kan-A-Di* at Binic·
- Good weather, calm sea
- Launch of 10 tons displacem length 10 metres (33 ft), Penta hp engines
- Anchors dropped from the s over a chain roller
- 8 mm chain of a fixed lengt 30 metres (16 fathoms) secured strongpoint in the centre of afterdeck
- Increasing tension obtained increasing the shaft revolution the launch engine
- Traction forces measured by mer tensiometer with compar reading
- Motor boat and underwater c eraman providing direct obse tion of events taking place on bottom
- Anchors painted yellow to prove their underwater visib and to aid in the detection after of the parts where greatest st had occurred
- Depth of water 3–5 metres 16 ft)
- Bottom fine homogeneous s of good cohesion.

(1) The trials of 22.8.79 were carrie out at Binic, in the Bay of St-Brieuc the Centre of Technical and Energy Studies of the Western Association Steam and Electric Appliances (APAVE), 5 rue de la Johardière, 44800 Saint-Herblain, France.

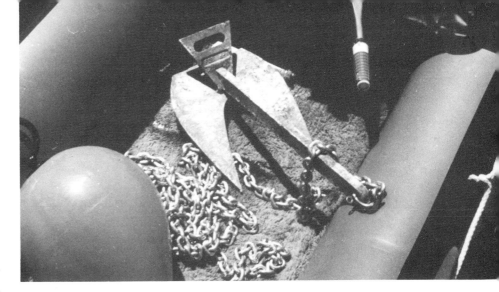

...way between Fob's old Bigrip and ...e Britany, the recent HPs scarcely ...d anything really new to available ...chors, unlike the CQR and Bruce when they first appeared.

Comments

...first trial, the only one we will
...with owing to the variety of
...els tested, produced
...surements of the force of
...stance to breaking out, and the
...e when being dragged, of
...n anchors. The figures inspire
...following comments:

...he Fob-HP would not break out
...e maximum traction available,
...kilos (2035 lb) (the report states
...the measurement was made
...he second trial, 'the first having
...n improperly carried out'). As a
...lt, its restraining force against
...g dragged could not be
...sured.

...he classic Britany, with
...racteristics very similar to those
...he Fob-HP, produced 780 kilos
...6 lb) of resistance before
...aking out, then 460 kilos (1012
...while dragging.

...he CQR is stated to have failed
...ake hold (280 kilos (616 lb)) on
...bottom. On the other hand it
...rgetically refused to drag,
...ducing a permanent resistance
...80–925 kilos (1716–2035 lb). In
...er words it proved its ability to
...d firmly even after having
...gged. I confess I cannot quite
...erstand the correlation
...ween these figures because, if it
...sts dragging with a force of 925
...s (2035 lb), how can it break out
...80 (616 lb)? . . .

...he Fisherman demonstrated
...t, without being dug in, it was
...dly able to obtain any useful
...d at this weight – which we
...w already.

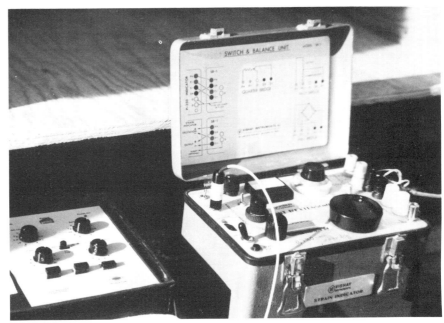

Comparative trials at St-Brieuc (August 1979)						
Anchor	Weight		Force to break out		Force when dragging	
1 Fisherman	12 kg	26½ lb	160 kg	352 lb	90/103 kg	198/226½ lb
2 Bruce	10 kg	22 lb	230 kg	506 lb	90/110 kg	198/242 lb
3 Old Fob	12 kg	26½ lb	275 kg	605 lb	110/135 kg	242/297 lb
4 CQR	11 kg	24 lb	280 kg	616 lb	780/925 kg	1716/2035 lb
5 Salle	12 kg	26½ lb	320 kg	704 lb	140/185 kg	308/407 lb
6 Britany MK-1	12 kg	26½ lb	780 kg	1716 lb	460 kg	1012 lb
7 Fob-HP	12 kg	26½ lb	925 kg	2035 lb	Not measured	

These five series of shots taken at Beg-Rohu throw significant light on the behaviour under traction of the anchors tested: the Maria-Theresa tumbling ineffectually onto its side; the remarkable burial of the CQR and the Britany with folding stock, which sank deeper into the bottom as the traction force increased; the overturning of the Britany MK-1 (without stock); the Fob-HP, which broke out from the bottom after a first traction, and then dug in again. (Photos ENV (National sailing school)

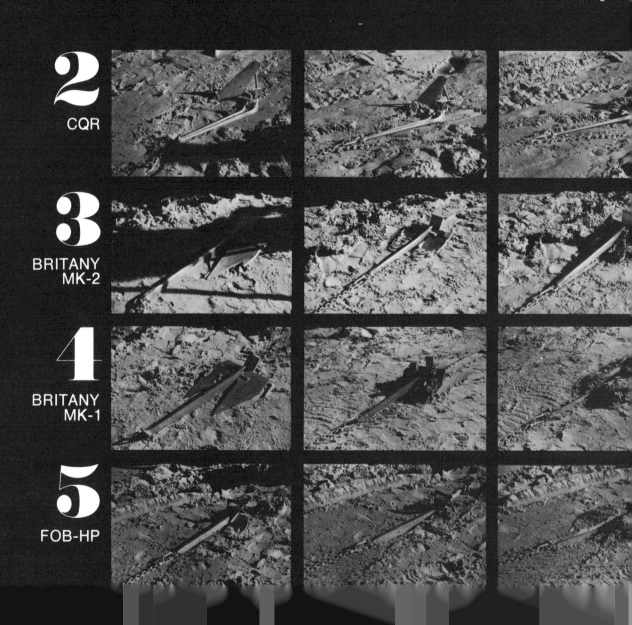

2 CQR

3 BRITANY MK-2

4 BRITANY MK-1

5 FOB-HP

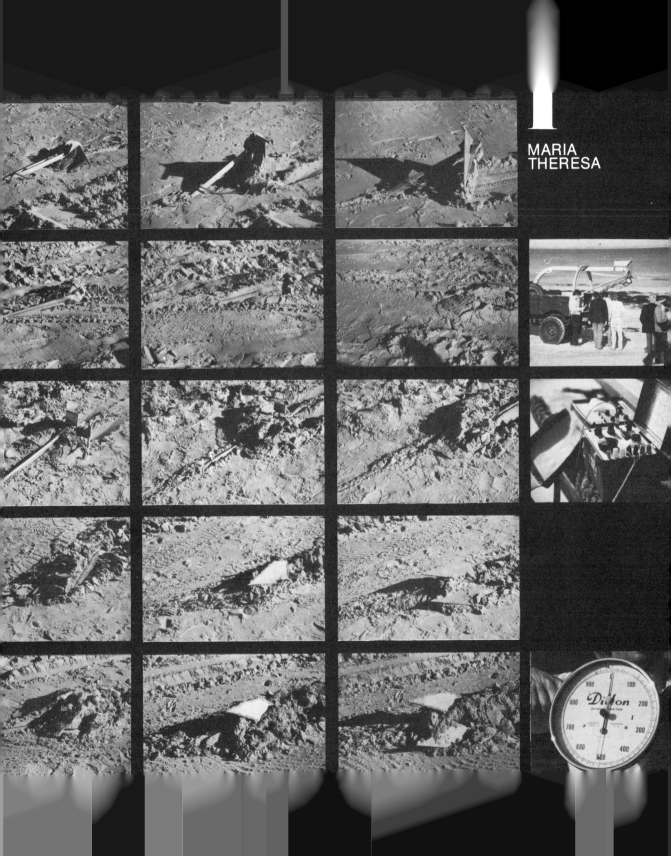

MARIA
THERESA

Conclusion

Trials which are commonly carried out produce a number of findings on the behaviour of anchors, under conditions which only reflect real-life situations to a very partial degree, for several reasons:

• only one type of bottom
• traction applied only in one direction
• force progressive and without jerks
• absence of important parameters such as swinging, shocks due to falling back on the chain through wind or swell, changed directions of pull, the difficulty of breaking out the most high-performance models after use under heavy traction, etc.

• the arbitrary choice of m(...) for comparative trials
• the limited number of tests (...)ing a trial, removing any possi(...) of averaging results under (...) chosen conditions
• the imprecise control ove(...) speed of movement of the sup(...) of the tractive force (and thus (...) force itself), which, as it may (...) falsifies the validity of the com(...)tive results
• the mechanical principle (...) which consists of subjecting (...) anchor to forces sufficient to (...) it out, normally a greater force (...) that to which they will be subj(...) under working conditions.

Alain Connan, conscious of t(...) fundamental problems, plans (...) to carry out new trials at Beg-R(...) which will take account of v(...) parameters more like those (...) with in real conditions of use, (...) on a more complete selectio(...) anchors (not provided by (...) manufacturer, he confided to (...) but obtained from the chandl(...) the corner, to avoid all selecti(...) source).

Indisputably, the position o(...) National Sailing School, rem(...) from all commercial pressures (...) provide an invaluable guarant(...) impartiality. Personally, I (...) much hope that the relevant M(...) try will come through with (...) necessary funds to allow this (...) ject to go ahead. I would even g(...) far as to lend them one of my (...) shackles!

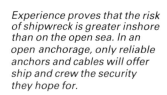

The forces acting on anchor and cable

Incontestably, our benevolent Administration in France reassures us by imposing strict quality norms on the manufacturers of anchors and their gear, and laying down rules for us, the users, when we are equipping our boats.

Thus we know that a sailing boat of 8 metres (26 ft) overall, if it does not exceed 3 tonnes, should have an anchor of 12 kilos (25 lb) shackled to a chain of 8 mm (5/16″) or a warp of 12 mm, the chain having a breaking strain of 4 tonnes and the warp only 3. Splendid. We know, on the other hand, thanks to the trials at Beg-Rohu and St-Brieuc, that a 12 kilo anchor will drag under an average traction of about 400 kilos (880 lb) (in the conditions under which the tests were carried out, of course). The first surprise is the difference between the two figures. But let us make some assumptions. Let us assume that we have the good luck to catch our anchor on a stray boulder, thus reinforcing the holding. One question then becomes more important than any other: what effort is finally going to be demanded of anchor and cable as the wind begins to show its teeth? Will it be 220, 1100 or 8800 lb of traction thrown against the cable during the strongest gusts? This seems to me to be a vital question, and I am amazed that not one book from among the wide-ranging collection

we keep in our ship's library even mentions these figures – not even approximately. It took me a long time and a great deal of research before I was able to bring together information from several different sources, all of which had been written by specialists for specialists.

This analysis has led me to construct a table applicable to all sailing boats in all wind strengths, from which an immediate reading can be derived of the wind pressure as a function of the exposed surface, and therefore the traction on the anchor, without complicated calculations or the need for a calculator.

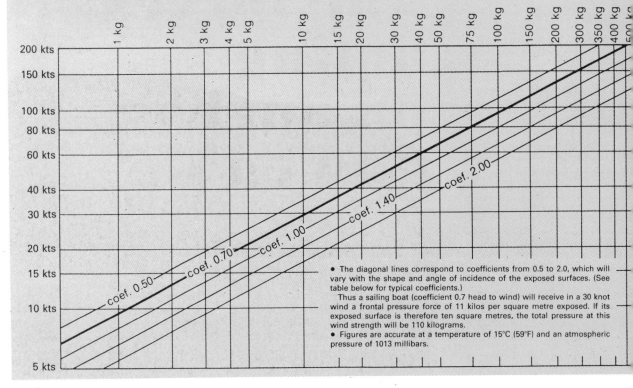

PRESSURE EXERCISED BY THE WIND ON A SURFACE (in kilos per square metre)

- The diagonal lines correspond to coefficients from 0.5 to 2.0, which will vary with the shape and angle of incidence of the exposed surfaces. (See table below for typical coefficients.)
  Thus a sailing boat (coefficient 0.7 head to wind) will receive in a 30 knot wind a frontal pressure force of 11 kilos per square metre exposed. If its exposed surface is therefore ten square metres, the total pressure at this wind strength will be 110 kilograms.
- Figures are accurate at a temperature of 15°C (59°F) and an atmospheric pressure of 1013 millibars.

The forces acting on an anchored boat derive from three different elements:

- windage
- effect of the current
- wave of action.

Each one of these parameters acts independently of the two others, but their forces can in certain circumstances work together, reinforcing or diminishing each other, as the case may be. When the wind pipes up in an open anchorage, they generally tend to reinforce each other, because of the common direction of wind and swell, which produce the most important forces.

Windage

This results from the combination of pressure and suction exercised by the wind on the freeboard of the hull, superstructures and rigging of a sailing boat. The force exercised depends on the wind speed, air density, and the shape and surface area of the object on which the aerodynamic pressure is exerted. Studied ever since 1686 (by Newton), this resistance to the flow of air has above all been calculated with great precision by aeronautical researchers. Wind-tunnel experiments, among others, have been carried out to obtain exact knowledge in this field. I will pass over the mathematical formulae which carry the physical phenomena into the realm of equations: it is easier to show by means of a table the coefficient of wind resistance according to the shape and profile of the exposed surfaces, which can then be applied to calculate the windage.

The following estimates, for a range of different types of object, provide a statistical base enough for it to be possible to sufficiently clear idea of aerod mic influences on windage (a which a good deal was kn already thanks to research b body designers). For objects sented face to wind:

SHAPE	COE
Concave hemisphere	1
Flat surface	1
Rigging wire, cylinder, mast	1
Cargo vessel (head-on)	0
Old-fashioned sailing boat	0
Tanker (head-on)	0
Modern sailing boat	0
Modern ferry	0
Modern motor launch	0
Sphere	0
Convex hemisphere	0
Commercial airliner	0
Aeroplane fuselage	0

...hen a good force 8 blows onshore ...an open anchorage, it is preferable ...away from the land before the sea ...ows us onto it. For of all the forces ...hich the anchor has to resist in bad weather, the strongest and most ...erous, are undoubtedly those of the waves and swell.

GRAF MONTFORT
HAMBURG

...mittedly these coefficients of ...tance are only estimates, the ...figure varying with the exact ...e of each object. For sailing ...s, which are our direct concern, ...oefficient lies between 0.7 and ...according to the shape of the ...the design of the superstruc-...s, and variable elements whose ...ce may be exposed, such as ...d foresails, badly furled main-...etc. In some cases these ...red sails can acquire resist-...characteristics similar to ...e of the concave hemisphere ...folds of the luff, for example) ...h make a major change in the ...ficient to be applied.

How to use this coefficient

...n I will leave aside the equa-...s, and offer merely a graph (see ...osite) giving a direct reading of ...value of windage per square ...e according to wind strength.

This is marked for coefficients from 0.5 to 2.0, with a heavier line for the 0.7 coefficient applicable to modern sailing boats (1). It will be noted that the resistance reaches about 12 kilograms per square metre in a 30 knot wind, rising to 42 kilos at 60 knots. This figure must be multiplied by the number of square metres of frontal surface exposed to obtain the total wind force acting on the anchored boat.

(1) Scientific note: normal variations in atmospheric density only affect the estimated forces marginally. It is still interesting to know the influence on windage resulting from changes in barometric pressure, temperature and humidity: high pressure increases air density; high temperature and humidity lower it. For a given wind speed, wind resistance will be greater on a cold, dry day than on a warm, humid one. This fact explains the special aggressiveness of some winter seas.

Example of the calculation:

For a yacht of just over 8 metres (26 feet) such as an Edel 820, the frontal surface can be broken down approximately as follows:

Hull	3.40 m^2
Mast	0.75 m^2
Sail	0.10 m^2
Rigging	0.25 m^2
Miscellaneous	0.50 m^2
Total	5.00 m^2

With a surface area of 5 m^2 head to wind, this yacht therefore produces a windage of approximately:

At 30 knots of wind:
12 kg/m^2 × 5 = 60 kg (132 lb)
At 60 knots of wind:
42 kg/m^2 × 5 = 210 kg (462 lb)

In theory, a 60 knot wind (severe storm force 11) would thus produce a traction force on the anchor cable of 210 kilos (462 lb) simply due to windage. This figure is interesting because at last it gives an idea of the forces imposed upon an anchor by bad weather. However, we must remember that a yacht in an open anchorage does not always lie exactly head to wind. The pressures exerted on the fore part of the hull, on furled jibs or on the main masts of ketches often cause a degree of yawing. This change of direction causes a change in the apparent surface, generally increasing it by a substantial percentage. The applicable coefficient will also be changed, because the surfaces in question are now less streamlined, being asymmetrical. These two factors can double the windage in extreme cases, so it is wise to consider that the windage figures obtained by the calculations above correspond to a minimum, which can be doubled when the boat yaws. So, for an Edel 280, we can say 200–400 kilos (440-880 lb) in force 11.

The way the ensign is streaming out from the stern of the catamaran (photo above) shows that a squall is approaching which may require some rapid veering of extra cable.

Dynamic pressure, in kilos, caused by wind on the frontal surface of modern sailing boat (Coefficient 0.7)

Frontal surface	10 knots	20 knots	30 knots	45 knots	60 knots	80 knots	100 knots	150
1 m²	1.2	4.5	11	25	42	75	120	2
2 m²	2.4	9	22	50	84	150	240	5
3 m²	3.6	13.5	33	75	126	225	360	7
4 m²	4.8	18	44	1100	168	300	480	1
5 m²	6	22.5	55	125	210	375	600	12
10 m²	12	45	110	250	420	750	1200	25
15 m²	18	67.5	165	375	630	1125	1800	37
20 m²	24	90	220	500	840	1500	2400	50

Force, in kilos, due to windage of a yacht of about 8 metres (26 feet) with frontal surface of 5 square metres

Wind in knots	10	20	30	45	60	80	100	15
Pressure in kilos	6	22	55	125	210	375	600	12

an variation of windspeed with height above sea level							
eight ove sea level	Windspeed in knots						
	10 kts	20 kts	30 kts	45 kts	60 kts	80 kts	100 kts
6 feet	8	16	24	36	48	64	80
16 feet	9	18	27	40	54	72	90
35 feet	10	20	30	45	60	80	100
55 feet	11	22	33	50	66	88	110
00 feet	12	24	36	54	72	96	120

This table shows how windspeed increases with height above sea level. Beaufort Scale measurements are conventionally taken at 35 feet above sea level, so real windspeed is greater at masthead height on a tall rig, whilst it will be marginally less at deck level.

Currents

force of the current flowing g the lines of a boat at anchor e same as that required to drive t that speed when under way. calculated in the same way, and gners can give the figures for eir hulls. For a modern yacht of about 26 feet, it is about:

- 20 lb (9 kilos) at 3 knots
- 37 lb (17 kilos) at 4 knots
- 64 lb (29 kilos) at 5 knots
- 119 lb (54 kilos) at 6 knots
- 297 lb (135 kilos) at 7 knots

urrents of 6 and 7 knots only r in very special places, it is that these effects will general-negligible outside a few high-dal areas. 37½ lb 17 kilos of tal traction for 4 knots of cur-being very small in compari-with windage figures.

Resistance to being driven		
Speed	6 m JI	NY 32
1 knot	2 kg	3 kg
2 knots	3 kg	9 kg
3 knots	10 kg	16 kg
4 knots	20 kg	25 kg
5 knots	30 kg	50 kg
6 knots	70 kg	82 kg
7 knots	200 kg	150 kg
8 knots	–	350 kg

The table alongside shows the theoretical forces required to drive two hulls, assuming calm water: that of a 6 metre J.I. (4.55 tonnes displacement for 7.59 metres waterline), and that of a New York 32 (11.38 tonnes displacement for 10.64 metres waterline), with the boat vertical. These figures correspond closely to the force exercised by a head-on current of the same speed.

with a heavy swell it will ... necessary to lengthen the cable ... considerable extent by the use ... hawser so that the total strain ... be only slightly increased, even ... gust, wave-crest and an extrem... yawing all occur together.

Conclusion

The traction effort imposed on ... anchor cable derives mainly fr... windage, unless the vessel is ... anchor in a rough and aggress... sea, in which case it is advisabl... reinforce the holding by lying ... two anchors, each with a sepa... cable (technically mooring), or ... backing up the main anchor wit... kedge attached to its crown. ... graph and tables on the preced... pages, by enabling the value of ... force to be calculated, give u... useful reference point from wh... to analyse the breaking-strain ... quirements of gear we may ... considering. The figures fin ... confirm that the forces impo... upon anchors during trials, exce... ing as they do the highest val... found in these calculations, do ... represent actual working con... tions in use. For the half-ton res... ance of a 25 lb CQR being drag... through the bottom correspond ... the traction created by a b... anchored in a 100 knot wind o... single anchor! As for the 8 ... (5/16") chain with its 4 ton break... strain, it is not from this that ... failure is likely to occur....

Wave forces

The situation is complicated by the forces produced by waves. Whether deriving from swell or actual waves, these forces can attain a momentary level of power which depends on four principal factors:

● the speed of water molecules carried along by a breaking wave
● the direct shock from its liquid mass against the hull
● the raising of the water level on the passing of a wave or swell crest, causing violent traction on the anchor cable
● the throwing backwards of the boat by the action of the seas, which can cause heavy snubbing.

The combined effect of these factors can often engender a force as strong as that from a severe gust of wind. Measurement with any accuracy is difficult, as yachts have periods of response to each of these oscillating factors, according to their design, size and weight. The strongest effect is that produced by the lifting of the bows under the action of swell. The only way to reduce this is to leave the boat as much freedom of movement as possible by increasing the scope and choosing a cable of great elasticity, which will reduce the peak force of the jerks.

In view of the individual nature of each case, it is impossible to provide accurate, general figures. My personal belief is that in bad weather, if the length of the scope corresponds to the state of the sea and the strength of the wind (that is to say, at least five times the depth of water for depths around five fathoms), then by using an all-chain cable the extra tension will be very limited in a sheltered bay, and its value will be very much less than the pull of the windage. On the other hand, in the open sea and

...ctical solution adopted on racing ...s is to stow the lengths of chain in ...stic bucket with handles, which, ...the boat has left coastal waters, ...e stowed below as low down and ...ntrally as possible to achieve better ...t distribution. Left Serenissima *...g a measurement session.*

Anchoring Equipment

...vards two o'clock in the morning, I ...awakened by squalls from the west ...ming in the rigging. Worried ab-...he holding, I quickly dug out my ...Fisherman from under a bunk and ...e haste to drop it on another chain, ...ard against the main anchor drag-...It is capable of holding a boat of ...imes my tonnage, so I returned ...idently to the warmth of my bunk.

...anchor held well; indeed, so well ...when at low water I wanted to raise ...move to another anchorage, I ...dn't shift it. The current, flowing at ...een five and six knots, held me ...n on to the wind, and at each gust ...ere nearly knocked flat. . . .

...very time the wind grew stronger ...the current, the chains were ...ned to breaking point, and my ...y warp was already chafing at the ...ead in spite of its bindings.

...ist as I was putting a third anchor ...the stern to control these danger-...yawings, an even more violent gust ...k and the chain was snatched ...ugh my hands. This chain was not ...e fast, because it is normally ...ed in the bows. I wanted to hang ...it at all costs, but it tore away the ...es of my canvas gloves, skinned ...ands and even took some flesh off ...fingers. In this temperature, heal-...vill be slow.' (1)

...though Marcel Bardiaux got ...y with nothing more than a ...d fright that night, his adven-

ture shows that the handling of anchors and their cables requires special equipment, more or less tailored to the size of the boat and the means of its owner. In this area, the indispensable minimum should be precisely adapted to the expected use; to make anchoring and weighing easier, protect equipment in use and ensure the greatest possible security. The positioning of gear also imposes constraints: chain lockers, anchor wells and lockers for secondary warps should be exactly right in the context of space available, with good ease of access and independent drainage.

A careful examination of the yachts displayed at the Boat Shows every year shows that far too many builders neglect these arrangements. The buyer of a standard production boat may therefore have to effect the installation himself. The problem should be studied with great attention before first going to sea, otherwise serious problems may arise.

(1) From To the Four Winds of Adventure *by Marcel Bardiaux, (Flammarion, 1958) from which the photograph on the right is taken.*

Stemhead roller

In almost universal use since the near total disappearance of bowsprits, the stemhead roller is fixed to the extreme bow of the boat. With single or double rollers, this piece of equipment has replaced the hawse hole which in the past was used on larger yachts (my old ketch *Nausicaa* had one, although she was only a 39-footer). Today one can see sailing boats of 80 feet and even bigger equipped with this useful embellishment, for reasons of convenience.

Advantages of the stemhead roller:
● being placed on the centre-line of the hull, which facilitates lateral movements of the cable while swinging
● providing open rollers on its upper side, easing the veering and recovery of cables in use
● being provided with large diameter rolling bearing points, which reduce friction and therefore the risk of chafing rope cables and the effort of recovery
● allowing the main anchor to be kept permanently secured firmly in its place on the stemhead, ready for instant use without fiddling about. Some double-rollers can even hold two anchors in position ready to drop.

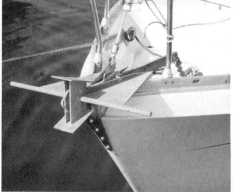

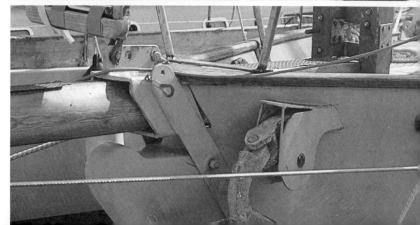

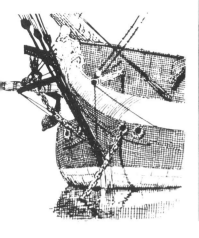

his last point is particularly
uable. In case of emergency, it
uld only take a few seconds to
ve anchor and cable ready for
. Take my word for it, there are
es in a cruising man's life when
sort of readiness can be of the
atest service.

ft, top to bottom:
CQR poised to torpedo the
derwater fauna. Well positioned
ng the centre-line of the stem, it
uld be solidly lashed down to
vent the shock of a wave or some
er untoward event from making it
np from the roller. Especially when
ling under spinnaker and mizzen
ysail!
The shank of this Danforth is
tainly going to be a nuisance when
ing to fix the tack of the jib under
y.
An excellent way of protecting the
ws from damage from the flukes of
anchor.
Hawse hole let into the bulwarks.
unusual idea, but consider the
eral strains when the boat is
ving. . . .

Anchor locks and lashings

It is important that when under way
the anchor on the stemhead should
be solidly secured. Leaving the
chain running through a fixed
windlass or around the samson
post is not enough. Close-hauled in
a rough sea, the waves take a
sneaky pleasure in releasing the
most firmly fixed gear. Some stemhead fittings have, as a complement to the system by which the
anchor is held by the shank by the
cable itself, a stainless steel bolt
which imprisons part of the anchor.
If your equipment does not have
such a lock, get into the habit of
securing the ring of the anchor to a
cleat with a security lanyard. This is
an ideal way to make the most
obstreperous bits of gear behave
themselves.

Even though a double roller here allows
two anchors to be kept in readiness,
the bobstay is always going to be a
great nuisance as the boat's head swings.
Left, foolproof samson post.

The samson post

Having been replaced by a windlass on boats of over about 30 feet
because of the weight of the chain
that has to be hauled up (nearly 10
lb per fathom for ⅜" – 9.5 mm),
samson posts are now generally
only found on smaller boats. This is
a pity, because they are very useful
in controlling the veering of a
second cable. The strongest samson post used to be a massive piece
of wood passing down through the
deck and stepped on the keel. For
reasons connected with making the
old type waterproof, or because of
the inconvenience to interior
arrangements, the samson post is
now usually metal, and bolted onto
the foredeck. It should be rein-
forced by a plate under the deck
(stainless steel, please) to spread
the strain over a wide area, because
the forces which will be applied to it
are considerable.

I would advise against the models with a horizontal bar running
through them from side to side, to
enable warps to be secured to them
in figures of eight: it is the most
effective known trap on a boat for
catching your ankles. . . .

Deck cleats

Mainly intended for mooring lines and warps, cleats on the foredeck are often called into service for securing the rope cables of secondary anchors. They can also be used for shock-absorbing systems which can be used on the chain in choppy anchorages to reduce the noise made as the boat swings about (we will return to this point later).

Size. It is also common, when in an open anchorage the anemometer begins to flirt with Beaufort forces in double figures, for these cleats to disappear under a confusion of cordage from different sources. So I would always insist that they should be oversize. Nobody has ever regretted having cleats too large, particularly on occasions when alongside, headropes, springs and breast ropes all need to be secured to the same cleat.

Position. Apart from their size, the positioning of these deck cleats should be a matter of careful thought. According to the optional equipment which you intend to fit, or your personal methods of manoeuvring, it may well be worth talking this matter over with the builder before construction starts. If too far inboard, they will encumber the foredeck, which always seems too small, making it hard to move around or preventing the forehatch or anchor well cover from opening properly. If right outboard they will tend to be buried under hastily lowered jibs, or be too far off the axis of the stemhead fitting. The answer is a matter of compromise and, above all, experience. That is,

as long as you have got th[e] before they have been fixed position.

Anchor cables and mooring warps should be carefully protected at the bearing points, especially where the pass through a fairlead or stemhead fitting. This is to protect them from chafe, which is always a problem in strong winds.

deep waters, the length of the usual anchor cable becomes too short. It must be lengthened, sometimes by 50 or 100 fathoms, to give the anchor a chance to get a hold before the cliffs of the coast are too near.

Hawsers

…se are the extra long ropes used … anchoring, mooring or when …ing out. The range of functions …ich they carry out during these …noeuvres calls for a number of …erent qualities and diameters. …sually kept for emergency use, …se ropes ought nevertheless to … immediately available, because …ir use will be required following … accident, or to prevent impend-… damage (we will return to this …ject soon). There will always … out to be too few of them, and …y will frequently be too short.

…n the course of my wanderings, I …e often taken a motor-driven …ghy to go to the help of yachts in …iculties, perhaps in an anchor-…e in bad weather, or when they …e grounded on an unexpected …al while under way. The lack of …ble warps aboard these boats … always astounded me: two …rps a few fathoms long, a single …hor hawser, and after that we …e to call in the genoa sheets or … spinnaker downhaul!

…he art of sailing is to think …ad. The most frequent cause of …nage to a boat is the contact of … hull with some form of solid …d. Few shipwrecks have any …er final cause. Having once been …own onto the rocks in heavy …ather, it is rare for the crew to be …e even to try to get the boat off

after the first impact, but when the grounding takes place in light weather or on a sandy bottom, the immediate use of anchors and hawsers adapted to the situation will often save the day. But speed is essential, for the tide may fall or the wind rise.

Basic Equipment

● 25 fathoms of nylon or terylene rope of the same diameter as that of the anchor warp
● 25 fathoms of nylon or terylene rope of slightly lesser thickness
● 50 fathoms of buoyant polypropylene rope of the same breaking strain as the anchor warp

---

The first and the third will be able to hold the boat even in violent wind: the second is used for various manoeuvres requiring less strength (1).

Note that the buoyancy of polypropylene offers extraordinary possibilities in certain circumstances; light, easy to tow when swimming or behind the dinghy, held up out of the way of propellers, it is my favourite type of rope for this kind of manoeuvres. *Pitcairn* has 100 fathoms permanently coiled in her lockers, in two lines of 20 mm diameter. Like lifeboats, they are only brought out on major occasions, but on those days they really are needed.

---

(1) See the table of rope characteristics on page 39.

Tripping lines

Although it has had other meanings in the past, this term now refers to the line which leads from the crown of an anchor to the surface of the water, to help in recovering it in case of difficulty.

The line should be made of nylon or terylene: *never* of buoyant polypropylene, which can cause accidents by floating up and catching in propellers. It can either be lead back aboard the boat along with the anchor cable, or it can run to a buoy designed to show the position of the anchor by floating vertically above it. We will look later at the exact method of using this particular piece of anchoring equipment.

Let us simply note that this tripping line is normally of thin line ($^5/_{16}$", or 8 mm, diameter is usual), as the strain to which it will be subjected is limited to lifting the anchor if it has jammed between two rocks or on some underwater obstruction. It would be hard to execute such a manoeuvre with enough force to break the line.

As its length may need to be that of the scope, it is prudent to carry some 10 to 15 fathoms of this line. It is unnecessary to equip the ends with eye-splices; here, as in so many shipboard uses, the bowline provides the greatest flexibility of use. As for the anchor buoy, it can

be of the classic ring and strop design (8–10 lb buoyancy is ample), or failing that, a fender will do perfectly well instead. But that is more of a temptation to marauding crews from other boats. . . .

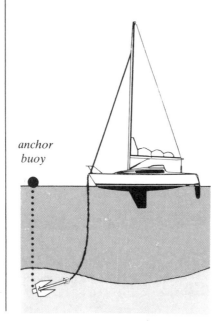

anchor buoy

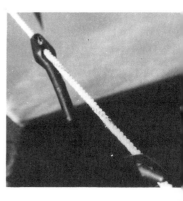

Rubber shock-absorbe

Made of ethylene-propylene rub moulded in one piece, they cush the shocks produced by the b snubbing against the cable. warp, fixed without using a kno wound round the shock-absor which, as it stretches under tension, lessens the violence of jerks, even so far as to absorb th completely.

The degree of the elastic mo ment, which varies with the chosen and the number of tu used, lies between 2 inches to v over a foot. The breaking strai as much as 7700 lb in the lar models, and there is no risk to boat as, even if the shock-absor fails, the warp remains intact. T type of gear is equally useful warps when moored alongside.

Needle and marline method for eye-splice on thimble

1) Pass the needle and marline through both ropes close to the thimble.
2) Sew the free end to the standing part.
3) Hammer the rope well into the thimble. Whip for half the length of the free end, and secure by passing through the standing part.
4) Complete the whipping and secure by sewing as shown.
(From the Marlow Guide.)

1

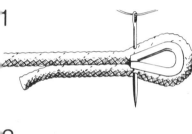

2

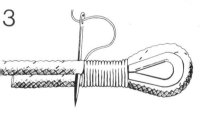

3

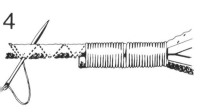

4

For those who think a bare minimum is all that is needed, here is the anchoring 'trousseau' which Bernard Moitessier put together for his *Joshua.*

Anchors

● One 84 lb Fisherman anchor with six fathoms of ⁷⁄₁₆″ (11.1 mm) chain and 30 fathoms of (22 mm) nylon. That was our working anchor.
● One 66 lb Danforth with 4 fathoms of ³⁄₈″ (9.5 mm) chain. This anchor was stowed on deck, lashed to the mainmast during coastal passages.
● A 22 and a 44 lb Fisherman and a 35 lb Colin Trigrip anchor, all three stowed in the bilges above the keel. Mainly intended for backing other anchors, but the Trigrip proved to be superior to the Danforth.
● One 88 lb Dial anchor, dismantled into three pieces so that it would stow on top of the keel ballast.
● One 55 lb CQR.

In my opinion, the CQR is the best anchor so far invented. After it, in order of preference (though this is still my personal opinion), comes the Fisherman, because it is an all-purpose anchor, and will not let you down suddenly, provided that its stock is long and its palms very large and pointed. Then comes the Colin Trigrip, which surprised me by its holding power and which I would use in preference to the Fisherman in tidal waters.

Chains

● 6 fathoms of ⁷⁄₁₆″ (11.1 mm) on the main anchor.
● 50 fathoms of ³⁄₈″ (9.5 mm) in various lengths, with a shackle already in place at each end so that they can be joined without loss of time rummaging through the shackle drawer.
● 30 fathoms of ½″ (12.7 mm). All these chains are stowed in the keel bilges, apart from the one for the main anchor.

Hawsers and Warps

● 30 fathoms of 22 mm nylon, making part of the main cable.
● 50 fathoms of 16 mm nylon rolled on a reel.
● 75 fathoms of 14 mm nylon rolled on a reel.
● 50 fathoms of 12 mm nylon.
● 100 fathoms of 8 mm nylon (50 fathoms on a reel).
● 50 fathoms of 6 mm nylon (for use as a tripping line).

Deck work aboard Endeavour I, *the J-class yacht designed by Charles Nicholson for Sir Thomas Sopwith in the hope of regaining the America's Cup at the time of the fifteenth challenge in 1934. If one cannot call upon the services of a crew of this quality (not always possible, after all), it is forgivable to resort to the discreet services of a windlass. Below right, the new manual Goïot model.*

Windlasses

Manual, electric, hydraulic or remotely controlled, there is a wide variety of windlass models for all tastes and needs. It is not at all necessary to have a sixty foot schooner to enjoy their good offices: there are models suitable for all sizes of boat. Certainly it is worth fitting one to any boat which uses chain of 5⁄16″ (8 mm) diameter or more. (Under French regulations, this means a yacht of 21 feet or which displaces a tonne or more.) The first quality of a windlass should be its robustness — which generally goes hand in hand with simplicity of design. In recent years, wider use has brought improved reliability thanks to the availability of stronger alloys, improved engineering and more permanent lubrication — usually by submerging the cogs in an oil bath.

There are three types of windlass:

• **Manual windlasses:** operated by a crank (single or double) or with the use of a double-action lever, these models have a drum for use with rope cables and gipsy designed to grip the chain. Some models offer only one of these alternatives, others have both on the same machine. The latter is more common. Better models allow the drum or gipsy to be used independently, and a system of ratchets ensures that warp or chain recovered cannot run out again. The provision of a friction brake and a retractable ratchet allows the gipsy to be released under control, permitting additional cable to be veered as desired.

The hauling force of manual windlasses varies from 550 to nearly 3000 lb for considerably less muscular effort.

● **Electric windlasses:** almost all with independent drum and gipsy, they offer the advantage of requiring no physical effort at all during anchoring operations, whether during the lowering or the recovery of the anchor. Their appetite is determined by the power of the motor which drives them: 1000 watts average for a lifting power of 1100 lb, 2000 watts for 2640 lb, with a hauling speed varying between 7 and 12 fathoms per minute according to make. This is reasonable consumption, but it is still advisable to have the engine (and therefore the alternator) running during prolonged use of the windlass. For chains of 5/16" to 3/8" (8 to 9.5 mm), 1000 watts power is sufficient (60–90 amps at 12 volts, 30–45 amps at 24 volts). A 2000 watt motor (50–60 amps at 24 volts, double at 12 volts) would only be needed for vessels using chain of 12 to 14 mm diameter.

Most electric winches are equipped to be remotely controlled.

The usefulness of Pitcairn's windlass more than makes up for the extra 35 lb of immoveable ballast fixed to the foredeck. Right, a sunken foredeck, accommodating a windlass neatly.

AVERAGE CHARACTERISTICS OF MODERN ELECTRIC WINDLASSES

Power	1000 watts	2000 watts
Lifting power	500 kilos	1200 kilos
Hauling speed	15 to 20 m/mn	20 to 25 m/mn
Consumption (12v)	60 to 90 A	100 to 120 A
Consumption (24 v)	30 to 45 A	50 to 60 A
Chain diameter	8 to 12 mm	12 to 14 mm

however, unless you boast a foredeck the size of Times Square, the
use of this accessory is most inadvisable, owing to the risks of
corrosion of the connecting cable,
or deterioration of the electrical
contacts due to salt water. A waterproof interruptor set into the foredeck near the pulpit is just as
convenient, and far more seaman-
like.

It is vital to complete the electrical installation by fitting a contact-
breaker adapted to the working
amperage, to prevent the motor
from burning out in the event of the
chain becoming fouled. Certain
models deal with this possibility by
the use of a 'mechanical fuse',
consisting of a drive belt connecting the gipsy to the motor's drive
shaft. If too much power is demanded from the machine, the belt will
give way before the motor is damaged. With this system, it is vital to
carry plenty of spare drive-belts.
and to be alert to what's happen-
ing.

As for the legendary fragility of
which this type of windlass is ac-
cused by its detractors, that is
only a measure of their inexperi-
ence. *Pitcairn*'s electric windlass
worked for seven years without
serious problem, coping with
several thousand miles of sailing
every season. I will not mention the
make, to avoid any controversial
matter being included in these
pages.

• **Hydraulic Windlasses**: mainly intended for use with chains of equal
or greater gauge than those mentioned above, and therefore for
large vessels. Driven by oil pressure, they require the installation of
pumps and complex circuits of pip-
ing, but their power can justify the
installation problems, as they offer
the very highest efficiency. Having
used one for five years, I can testify
that nothing will stop them except
the breakage of a component. For
handling by experts only!

• **Capstans**: used on smaller
boats, these combine the functions
of windlass and samson post. Unlike a windlass, a capstan works in a
vertical axis on which a drum
(usually grooved) is mounted,
sometimes with a gipsy underneath, as in this example above.
Worked either manually, with a
lever and ratchet, or electrically, the
manual variety is increasingly
being replaced by a simple winch.
For myself, I prefer the manual
windlass, with its more specific
purpose.

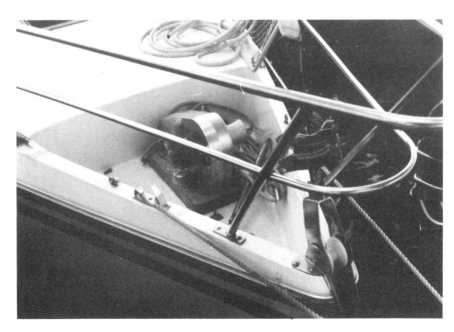

When he cast off from Boston on his legendary circumnavigation, Joshua Slocum was 51 years old, and his Spray *twice as old again. It was after he had coasted down the west coast of America that he met the first williwaw squalls.*

The *Spray* under sail

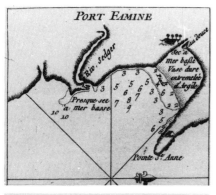

'On the morning of the 9th, after a refreshing rest and a warm breakfast . . . the day to all appearances promised fine weather and light winds, but appearances in Tierra del Fuego do not always count. While I was wondering why no trees grew on the slope abreast of the anchorage, half minded to lay by the sail-making and land with my gun for some game and to inspect a white boulder on the beach, near the brook, a williwaw came down with such terrific force as to carry the Spray, with two anchors down, like a feather out of the cove and away into deep water.

'The second day, I had no sooner gotten to work at sail-making again, after the anchor was down, than the wind, as on the day before, picked the sloop up and flung her seaward with a vengeance, anchor and all, as before.

'I had the sloop soon under good control, however, and in a short time rounded to under the lee of a mountain, where the sea was a smooth as a mill pond and the sails flapped and hung limp while she carried her way close in. Here I thought I would anchor and rest till morning, the depth being

eight fathoms very close to the ⌐
But it was interesting to see, as I ⌐
the anchor, that it did not rea⌐
bottom before another williwaw ⌐
down from this mountain and ⌐
the sloop off faster than I could p⌐
cable. Therefore, instead, of res⌐
had to "man the windlass" and ⌐
up the anchor with fifty fatho⌐
cable hanging up and down in ⌐
water. This was in that part of the⌐
called Famine Reach. Dismal F⌐
Reach! On the sloop's crab-wind⌐
worked the rest of the night, th⌐
how much easier it was for me w⌐
could say, "Do that thing o⌐
other," than now doing all mysel⌐
I hove away and sang the old ⌐
that I sang when I was a sailor. ⌐
the last few days I had passed th⌐
much and was now thankful th⌐
state was no worse. It was day⌐
when the anchor was at the haws⌐

(*Extract from* Sailing Alone A⌐
the World *by Joshua Slocum.*)

84

The foredeck is the most exposed area aboard a sailing boat. Whatever type of anchor-raising equipment is chosen, it should be remembered that it will be continuously put to the test by sea water. Avoid remote control systems on electric capstans and windlasses; they will hardly last the length of one spring tide.

Anchor Ball

International regulations demand that a vessel at anchor shall exhibit a black ball of diameter at least 60 centimetres (say 2 ft). It is worth noting that several 'anchor balls' are on sale which measure less than the minimum size. In practice, this rule is very often ignored by pleasure craft in a number of countries, as indeed is the cone which should be displayed when a yacht is motor-sailing.

One wonders for how long the various authorities will remain so tolerant about the infringement of these regulations. Apart from the risk of action taken merely because of failure to display, there is also the risk that if an accident were to happen, say through collison or the fouling of an anchor warp, failure to show the proper signal might be grounds for an accusation of contributory negligence. This is without mentioning insurance policies, all of which have clauses invalidating the policy if the vessel is in breach of official regulations. So watch out! Even if you claim that you had just mislaid the ball, you may find that your insurance company is not very flexible about such absent-minded instances.

Anchor Lights

en at anchor outside a port, a
sel must show an all-round
te masthead light, visible 5
es for vessels between 50 and
metres in length, 3 miles for
12 metres, or 2 miles for boats
ler 12 metres. It should be rec-
ised that, regulations apart, this
al adds an important element
security in some busy anchor-
s. I remember (and this would
October, 1980), anchoring *Pit-
n* in a sheltered creek in the part
he Spanish coast that lies be-
en Valencia and Gibraltar, away
n any built-up area and only a
boat's lengths from a wild and
olate shore. In view of all these
ors, I didn't bother to hoist a
t. You can just imagine the leap
ich took me on deck when, at
ut two o'clock in the morning,
rumble of an engine running at
ximum power thundered out of
night: close by, and sounding
powerful as a tank. In the event,
urned out to be only a local
ning boat that had come to take
lter a hundred yards from us,
iting until the wind eased. They
st have been rewinding one of
ir long lines onto its reel, using
throttle to show everyone how
d they were working. After turn-
on my masthead light to guard
inst a possible second act to the
ma, I returned to my bunk, my

*Although not always complied with on
sailing boats owing to the amount of
current consumed, the regulation for
vessels at anchor is as follow: up to 50
metres (165 ft) in length, an all-round
white light. Larger vessels, all-round
white lights bow and stern, the light in
the bow being placed higher than the
after light.*

temples still beaded with retrospec-
tive sweat.

Admittedly, a light with a visibility of two or three miles is bound to
use a fair amount of current. For
those whose batteries are not too
keen on that sort of drain, there are
two other possibilities:
● A portable electric lantern of lesser power. This will still be sufficient to draw attention to your
position at closer range, which is,
after all, the important thing.
● A paraffin (kerosene) fueled hur-
ricane lantern, so designed as to
remain alight even in wet or windy
conditions.

These lights are suspended from
the forestay by a foresail halyard,
about half-way up from stem to
masthead. They can save your
boat, or at least protect your sleep,
particularly when the noise of the
wind in the rigging masks the
sound of another vessel coming
dangerously close.

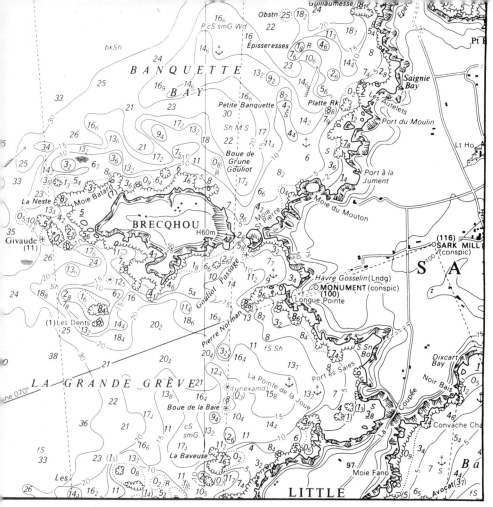

The new printing methods of the hydrographic authorities provide a great advance in clarity with their colours and high-quality printing, it is impossble not to regret the old ones with their hachuring and fulle indications of bottom composition The differences can be seen in thes examples. If the chart doesn't tell y what you want to know, and there no hand lead aboard, the only remaining solution . . . dive!

The hand lead

Sounding with a lead is hardly ever seen aboard modern yachts, as the convenience offered by an echo sounder (still very cheap compared with other electronic navigation aids) has almost entirely relegated the lead to the ranks of relics of another century. It must also be admitted that the use of the lead, immobilising an experienced crew-member at a time when all hands are usually fully employed (arriving at an anchorage), can often present problems, especially when short-handed already.

The *real* usefulness of the lead is more usually after the anchor has been dropped, in order to find out the exact nature of the bottom, because, in spite of the claims made by some makers and di butors, echo sounders sold yachts do not indicate this nearly enough accuracy: and ne er does the chart. Only the bott sample brought to the surface the layer of tallow in the hollow the bottom of the lead will tell whether the bottom here is cove by weed, gravel, rocks, sand mud.

This is information of the utm importance, as we shall soon s in determining the choice of ca and anchor, length of scope number of anchors needed assure the best degree of safety boat and crew. In France, indee is compulsory to carry a hand l on most cruising boats, and course it can be vital in the even a failure of the echo sounder.

Left, digital readout provided by a Lowrance model for cockpit fitting. Right, from top to bottom, rotary sounder fitted above the chart table with external repeater (this is the one aboard Pitcairn*). Centre, the Plastimo Shark. Below, the Mironga, made by Pen Lann with an integral calculator, and the Royal NF-320, combined rotary neon and recording, for searchers for wrecks.*

The echo sounder

apparatus is grouped with the
nd steering compass as one of
hree most precious navigation-
ds on our boats: indeed, prob-
the only really useful ones. In
rast to the hand lead, it pro-
s instantaneous and con-
us information without taking
e time of a crew member. Its
is indispensable throughout
various phases which precede
ctual letting go of the anchor.
equally necessary to enable the
ired scope to be calculated, as
is directly proportional to the
h of water under the hull. I will
ne myself in this chapter to
ribing the characteristics of the
rent types of echo sounder
able on the market, which are
ving more numerous every
, though they all have much the
e qualities.

Principal models:

otary neon **sounders**. These are
most common. A revolving
light flashes at a point on its
lution indicating the depth.
e are usually two scales, some-
s 0–60 feet and fathoms, some-
s 0–20 and 0–100 metres.
lly reasonably priced.

igital **sounders**. New. The
h is indicated directly by a
e on a screen.

ecording **sounders**. Four or five
s the price of the above, they

trace the profile of the bottom on a graduated paper strip (in metres or foot) as a continuous tracing, on the desired scale.
• **Options** on the first two types mentioned above:
(1) Repeater in the cockpit.
(2) Alarm, set off automatically when the depth falls to the figure to which the machine has been set.

Most low-powered sounders, especially rotary neon models, are fed either by torch batteries or from the boat's 12 or 24 volt main supply. In view of the constant use to which the equipment is put in coastal cruising, I advise the second alternative, which removes the risk of flat batteries at a crucial moment. As for the recent developments mentioned above, I regard the alarm (single or double) as a selling gimmick rather than a really useful service. *Pitcairn* has had one for five years, but I have only used it to amuse visitors while in port. Although this permanently alert sentinel may seem a wonderful idea in theory, in practice it is seldom worth the bother of setting it.

What does seem to me to be important is for the helmsman to have a repeater on which he can read the depth, day or night. With only two people aboard, one on the foredeck, the other at the helm, it is no use having to dive below every ten seconds in order to find out the depth at the moment of anchoring. For this reason, the cockpit repeater is undeniably useful.

Polaroid Glasses

raise your eyebrows and look
surprised: polarised sunglasses
are precious allies when dodg-
ing among the shallows looking for
ce to anchor. I find them so
that I have often wondered
the lookout men of Cook,
ainville or La Pérouse man-
to guide their heavy sailing
through the reefs of the
n Seas without them.
theless, it appears that, in
of the lack of charts and
g directions, these pioneers
went aground. No doubt
crews had better trained
ght than ours and, from the
t of the crow's nest, a perch
favourably placed for observ-
e underwater world. But cer-
since I first discovered the
of Polaroid filters in coastal
ng, I have experienced the
feeling of sharpness of vision
ne feels in winter at the wheel
car after wiping the mist from
indscreen. By suppressing the
ce reflections, these glasses
the eye to see down into the

water to observe the contours of
sandbanks or pick out areas of rock
on the bottom. Hundreds of times I
have seen crew members with
polarised glasses pointing out to
the others a shoal marked on the
chart, which makes it clear that they
are the only ones who can see
below the surface with any clarity.

I need hardly say that for inspect-
ing the approaches to an anchorage and checking over the swinging circle, these little-appreciated
accessories do wonders. So much
so that I do not hesitate to include
them on my list of favourite navigational instruments.

*Polarising filters used in photography,
by reducing reflections, improve the
view under water, just as Polaroid
sunglasses do.*

2 Part Two
ANCHORING
TECHNIQUES

The search for shelter

the best-performing and most
fully selected anchoring gear is
enough to assure security in a
or anchorage. To achieve that,
also necessary for the gear to
used competently, taking into
unt the infinitely variable fac-
of place, weather and circumst-
. The options available to a
per who wants to stop for shel-
are numerous, especially if
e is no formal harbour avail-
. He must make a precise
ce, after which it will be dif-
t, if not impossible, to change
mind without weighing anchor
n. Taking account of the direc-
of wind and swell, he therefore
to determine as quickly as
ible:

- an area of sheltered water
- the exact place to anchor
- the nature of the bottom
- the anchor and cable to be
  used
- the length of the scope
- any necessary further precautions.

rrying out these calculations
ires common sense as much
xperience. And indeed a good
of skill, when the anemometer
s like going off the scale!

day is dying, the sea is building
our by hour, it is time to seek
er somewhere along the already
ening coast before the bad
her arrives.

Without the pressure of doing it
for real just now, let us examine
each phase of the operation in
detail. We won't put our nose out of
harbour until we have finished the
chapter. So let us consider the
problems.

WHERE SHALL WE ANCHOR?

Finding an area of sheltered water
is of primary importance. On its
calmness will depend the comfort
of the anchorage, allowing a reduction in the fatigue imposed upon
boat and crew. Protected from
waves or swell, they will have only
the assault of the wind to contend
with, and sometimes this may be
reduced by the protection afforded
by the land. Only sometimes,
though, because valleys may actually funnel the wind and increase the
severity of the squalls. At this point,
a study of the chart will suggest
which option to choose, taking into
account various factors according
to prevailing conditions:

- visibility
- wind direction and force
- direction of waves or swell
- weather forecast
- distance to alternative
  shelter
- time of sunset
- length of proposed stay
- special problems.

So we are faced with choosing a
geographical zone, near or further
off, whose position appears favourable in the light of the present and
foreseen direction of the wind, and
therefore in general the swell. Once
the general choice has been made,
other criteria are added to the fore-
going ones to enable the most
sheltered corner of the anchorage
to be chosen, either from the chart
or sometimes actually on arrival:

- difficulties in the approach
- depth of soundings
- characteristics of the tide
- aspects of the land
  geography
- ease of leaving by night.

This is a lengthy list, and we are
going to go through it item by item.
It is well worth the trouble.

95

First approach

● **Visibility** At night or in poor visibility, approaching the coast always involves a certain danger, particularly in the absence of buoys or beacons (almost always the case away from ports). In this situation any attempt to anchor should be avoided: stay at sea until visibility returns or, if some important problem requires an urgent return to land, look for a buoyed channel. In thick fog, a course set for a well-buoyed area is the least perilous, although one can hardly say the safest, way to approach land. This is on condition that the marks are clearly identifiable, so that they will guide your subsequent course to the chosen shelter without risk of grounding.

At night, navigational lights and those of the land will sometimes make it possible to find the way into a bay. For this, the soundings must be suitable, the boat's searchlight must be capable of cutting through the darkness for two or three hundred yards, and the conditions of wind and current must limit the risks to a minimum. This sort of attempt should only be made under power, and if the skipper has a solid background of experience. Otherwise, set course for deep water, or heave to and set watches on deck. Wait for daylight.

Right: We are cruising to the south of Budelli when the evening weather forecast announces a gale warning from the east. There can be no doubt: the best shelter is in the deep bay on the north coast of the island, protected by a steep hill to windward.

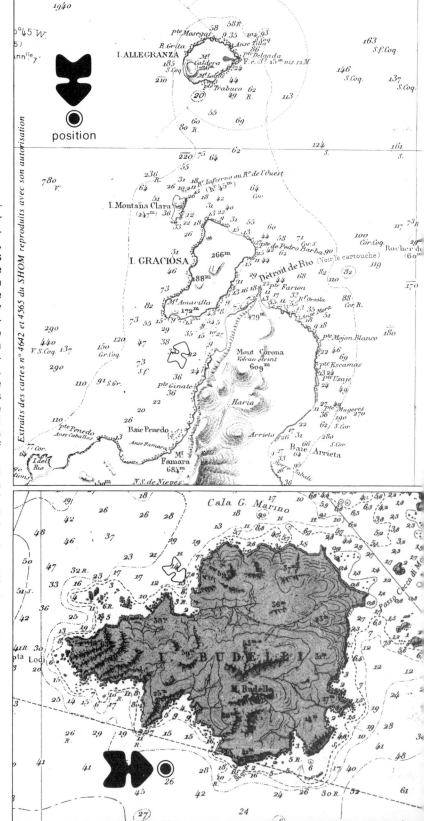

; you find yourself southwest of *granza in the Canaries, and want* *ichor to shelter from a strongish* *herly wind. No use hoping for any* *fort in the lee of Allegranza or* *itana Clara: the swell will run* *t round both of these islands. The* *turbulent shelter will be found* *g the south coast of Graciosa; it* *certainly be rough at the exit from* *'trait, but the shore is indented* *igh to provide a bay protected* *t the swell somewhere along its* *th.*

Wind direction and force Nine es out of ten it will be the ection of the wind that deter- es the most sheltered area. On ig island, this will normally be ng the coast downwind from the d; for a coast exposed to the nents, it may be in an interior , an estuary, or under the lee of eninsula. The examples oppo- give a good idea of this phase he research, and how the chart uld be examined in the light of meteorological situation. Re- nber that, although the wind sometimes ease under the ter of a weather shore (we shall rn to this point later), the im- tant thing is not so much protec- from the wind itself as from the es created by its action on the

Direction of waves or swell s will be governed by the ngth of the wind, the length of e for which it has been blowing, the extent of the area of water acting upon (the fetch). Waves always governed by the ngth and direction of the wind ving at the time; swell, on the er hand, can be residual, or the cursor of a far-off gale. In other 'ds, it may be from a local wind t has now moved away, or from earby one that has not yet ved. In such cases, it is possible

for the direction of the waves form- ing the swell to be different from that of the wind at the time, in which case protection may be needed from waves moving in two different directions. Apart from these special situations, it is usually enough to get into the shelter of a weather shore for the sea condi- tions to improve.

● **Weather forecast** Shipping or other forecasts, or the observation of the barometer, the sky and the swell, can all give notice of an approaching change in the weath- er, and therefore sea conditions. This must be taken into account when deciding on an anchorage, as the present conditions may be totally changed during the hours to come. Thus, in Provence, the easterly gale which often follows the *mistral* (a strong NW wind in those parts) can produce great dis- comfort in anchorages chosen merely with a view to protection from the northwest. Similar prob- lems can be met with at Le Palais, when a westerly breeze that has been established for days is often reversed in the middle of the night by a nor'easter, unless one has foreseen the change in wind and anchored accordingly. The art of sailing is made up of details of this kind which, I would mention in passing, make up a lot of its charm. Even if it sometimes finds you on

the foredeck weighing anchor by moonlight in your pyjamas, be- cause the rocks that were to wind- ward when you turned in are now close a-lee under your stern. Later, you can get back below and dream of a house in the country with granite foundations. . . .

● **Distance to alternative shel- ter** This is a factor whose import- ance will vary with the time of day, extent of the detour involved, and the speed of the boat (not to men- tion the influence of the tidal streams the next day, which may give you an additional advantage or disadvantage). Always bear in mind that beating along a coast to windward takes two or three times as long, tiring the crew prop- ortionally, as running the same distance downwind. Especially once the sea has built up.

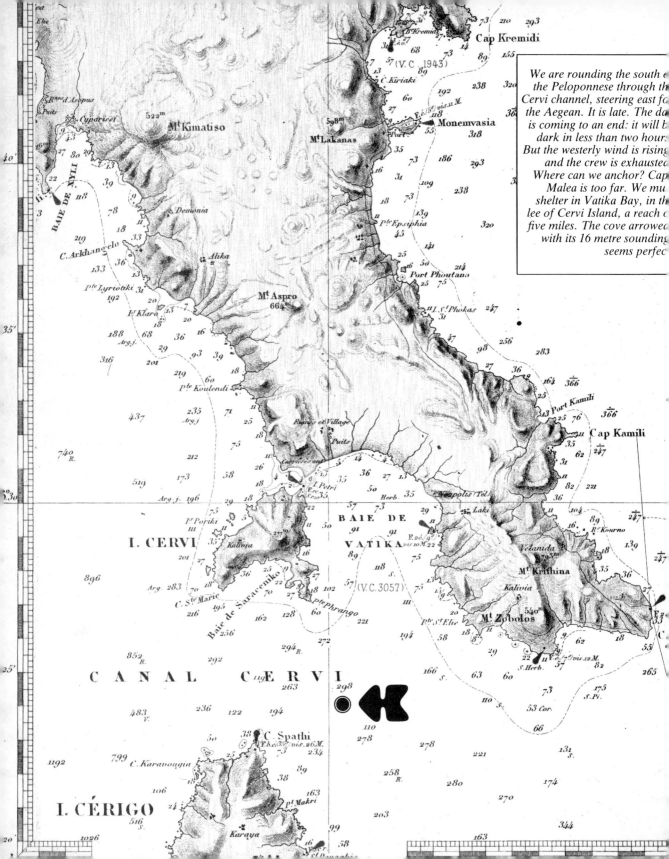

We are rounding the south e
the Peloponnese through th
Cervi channel, steering east fo
the Aegean. It is late. The da
is coming to an end: it will b
dark in less than two hours
But the westerly wind is rising
and the crew is exhausted
Where can we anchor? Cap
Malea is too far. We mu
shelter in Vatika Bay, in th
lee of Cervi Island, a reach o
five miles. The cove arrowe
with its 16 metre sounding
seems perfec

...airn, in the Straits of Bonifaccio, ...ring between the two islets of the Corcelli archipelago. A quiet ...chorage in a bend in the sound protected from NW gales.

...ime of sunset This is directly ...d up with the factors in the last ...graph. Experience shows that ...pproach to land, identification ...ndmarks and passage to the ...orage always take longer than ...calculated while at sea. I know ...from experience, these land-...between evening and night, ...eye on the rocky headland ...ening the anchorage, the other ...e compass with a searchlight ...g over the shoulder, and details ...e chart etched into the mem-

...1920 the anchor goes over the ...in the last glimmer of dusk, the ...are furled by torchlight, the ...sounder and the beam of the ...chlight provide the sole, in-...uate, indications about the im-...ate environment. At 2010, a ...nd anchor is laid out if the ...lls go on: then sleep claims ...the most enduring crew mem-...At last, after a final inspection ...e anchor cables, which he ...hens by a few metres for extra ...rity, the skipper casts a last ...e at the barometer, and at ...imitates his companions. He ...et up several times during the ...., checking on the swinging ..., making sure that no reef or ...l is lurking in the vicinity. ...vellous anchorage!' he will ...ater. 'Quiet as anything, per-...shelter. Funny though, there ...something worrying about ...night. . . .'

● **Length of proposed stays**
This will have great influence on the choice of anchorage. Clearly, for a mid-day stop of a few hours, for lunch or a bit of underwater fishing in good weather, the precarious shelter of an open bay may be fine. These brief stops are all part of the fun of coastal cruising, when the sun is shining down on clear water. But much greater security is needed if the boat is to spend a night in an anchorage, even more so if it is to be for several days. A major change in the wather may occur during such a period, so an anchorage must be chosen that will provide shelter from all the main prevailing winds (their directions will be found in the pilot books): a really snug position.

● **Special problems** Rigging failure, motor breakdown, lack of provisions, dental crisis or bodily accidents are the sorts of thing that may require a landing as soon as

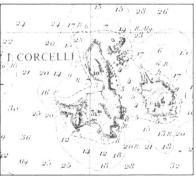

possible; and in a place which provides a solution to the particular problem. Admiralty pilot books and yachting pilots (backed up by land-based tourist guides) will provide precious information about local resources in such cases. As every situation presents its own individual features, it is up to the skipper to decide on the strategy to adopt, according to the urgency of the situation. Ease of getting ashore might thus, for instance, take priority over the comfort of the anchorage.

Chart, right: we are approaching St Martins in the Scilly Islands, in a moderate westerly breeze. As west winds are the most usual in this area, we decide to anchor either in St Martins Bay or at the head of Bread and Cheese Cove, on the island's NE coast. The first haven is bigger, but its approach is less clearly visible than the second, which has two easily identifiable landmarks on either side of its entrance: Burnt Hill and the St Martins Head beacon. Let us make an immediate note of the course for leaving: 348° Magnetic, with the open Channel less than a mile away.

Final approach

That is all for the first phase of the research, in which the most favourable general area for anchorage is decided upon. Now we have to take the more detailed decisions, whose study will be carried out with documents in hand. First on the detailed chart of the area chosen (on the largest scale possible), then with the help of the navigational works carried aboard for the purpose: pilot books (even though they may not be very informative about the sort of anchorages we are interested in), tide tables, yachtsmen's pilots, articles from yachting magazines, etc. There can never be too many of them, for, as each is generally incomplete, it is usually necessary to pool all the available information before one can solve the whole puzzle.

To decide the exact position where the boat is to be anchored, a number of factors have to be considered. Let us go through the list which was set out above:

● **Difficulties in the approach** Underwater reefs, coastal dangers,

offshore rocks, violent currents, lack of clear landmarks to help identify the landfall . . . the list of traps which lie in wait for the navigator approaching land is as long as a windless day. It is when trying to take account of them and to work out courses and transits designed to keep us out of trouble that we regret not having the largest scale chart aboard (but considering their prices nowadays, it is understandable that users cannot afford to buy them all). The spot chosen should therefore be one where position can be *accurately* judged, as the least error, by modifying the underwater environment, can bring the risk of the appearance under the bow of a submerged rock not mentioned on the chart. In bad weather, that is all that is needed to add one more to the list of famous shipwrecks.

Always, if a known danger exists near the entry route, try to pass to leeward of it. If this is impossible, leave as much room as possible between it and the boat, to avoid being carried down on it immediately if something goes wrong – a recipe for instant disaster. (A principle of conduct which any skipper worthy of the name will abide by at any time when passing close to a hazard.)

● **Depth of soundings** These will be judged according to the draft of the boat, and the variations in

depth caused by the rhythm of tides in areas where this appl For less experienced navigators wise, in Channel and Atlantic ters, to consider the soundings the chart to indicate the maxim depth at low water, even at ne tides. That way you will safegua the underwater fauna, avoidi leaving a trial of fish paste all o the bottom, and you will a escape the need for complicat calculations. This only applies this stage of the research, as shall see later that the range of tide is an important factor in calculation of the scope of cal needed.

It is important to note that wh all modern European (includi British) charts show soundings metres on a chart datum of Low Astronomical Tide (LAT), many tions have not yet been chang and some give soundings fathoms or feet, and in some cas chart datum is still mean low wa springs (MLWS), in which ca there can be considerably less ter than charted at an extre spring. Even more importa charts of the Kattegat and the B tic, from whatever source, based on a datum of mean lev and under certain conditions wind and tide the actual level fall to one metre or more bel chart datum.

● **Land geography** Apart from providing landmarks to help recognise the approach to the anchorage, the relief of the coastline around the haven will have a direct influence on the characteristics of the wind to be found there. According to the height of the land, its irregularity and the direction of any valleys which may cut through it, the hinterland will produce local increases or decreases in the strength of the squalls experienced. I remember being caught in a *meltemi* while we were trying to beat our way up to Mykonos, a small island in the Aegean. With a rising sea, we were glad to drop anchor at the head of a creek in the mountainous island of Nicaria, especially as the strength of the gusts increased from the 35 knots we had been experiencing at sea to 50 knots close to the land. 'What must it be like outside!' thought Monique and I, as we tripled our anchors.

After three days of incessant squalls which transformed the anchorage into a witches' cauldron, we weighed anchor, determined to get on our way whatever happened, regardless of the heavy weather. Surprise: as soon as we got away from the island, the anemometer unwound by two forces Beaufort, settling back onto the regular 35 knots that we had had until we approached the land. Still plenty, but a strength you have to learn to live with in the Mediterranean (or else change your cruising ground!) Funnelling between peaks or compressed by a sudden cliff, the force of the wind can thus be considerably increased by the venturi effect. On the other hand, a low isthmus or an extent of flat land to windward will have little effect on the behaviour of the wind. It can be reduced under the protection of a jagged mountainous barrier, or upwind from a steep cliff; but it is impossible to generalise too widely, as the study of this complex phenomenon consists very largely of special cases.

● **Ease of night departure** Nothing is worse than feeling oneself to be trapped in the grasp of a closed-in bay while the anchors steadily drag under the assault of the squalls. It has happened to me: principal cable parted and second anchor rattling over the coral at the speed of a Saturn rocket. And no one to ask which way is out!

The trouble is, the safer the anchorage, the more likely this problem is to appear. Above all, avoid those little mouseholes with reef-encrusted entrances, especially if the holding has proved defective during the day. For my part, a glimpse of open horizon over the stern makes me sleep better in an anchorage. *Much* better.

So now we have decided exactly where we are bound, let us say a few miles away. The boat slips into sheltered water, the deck still wet with the spray from the open sea. The crew are dead tired, but happy at the thought of the mug of hot coffee which each of them will soon be enjoying in a cockpit which has at last stopped moving about, and is dry!

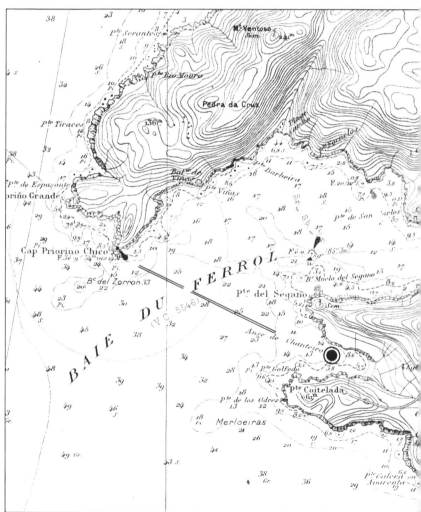

A bit of luck one rarely encounters: a lighthouse on the exit course from an anchorage, to guide a night departure – as long as there is no fog.

The study of the large-scale chart [shou]ld be carried out meticulously, to [de]termine with the greatest possible [p]recision the possible dangers, the [d]epths in approach and anchorage, [a]nd the nature of the bottom if this is given.

[PR]EPARING TO ANCHOR

[Betw]een the moment when the [skipp]er decides upon his anchor-[age] and the anchor touching the [bott]om, a number of operations [mus]t be carried out to ensure the [man]oeuvre the greatest possible [chan]ce of success. To set out these [operation]es as clearly as possible, we [will b]egin by assuming that arrival [will] be under power. Arrival under [sail] will be left until later, after we [have] analysed the general princi-[ples] of the technique of anchoring. [Be]ar in mind that even the most [eleg]ant manoeuvre is seldom more [than] a step away from disaster!

[Cl]earing the decks As there is [neve]r enough room on any fore-[deck], it is vital that it should be [clear]ed of all superfluous equip-[men]t. The jib should either be bag-[ged] and stowed in the forepeak, or [lash]ed to the lifelines if the skipper [prefe]rs to keep it hanked on. In the [latte]r case, the tack should be re-[leas]ed and the hanks raised as high [as po]ssible above the deck: a cord [aroun]d the pulpit usually serves [admi]rably. Also check that the spin-[nake]r downhaul is out of the way, [and] that the forehatch is properly [clos]ed.

● **Selection of the crew member in charge of handling the anchoring gear** Preferably experienced, and familiar with the gear he will be using, he must know in advance how to veer cable, stop it on demand, let out a bit more or recover some of the slack as required. On a boat of greater tonnage, these operations can involve real dangers: remember Alain Colas' accident at La Trinité, so there is a case for giving the most experienced crew member this task.

● **Dress** The crew member must wear boots, and preferably gloves, especialy in the case of a woman. When working close to a windlass, beware of over-large clothing or oilskins, with flapping sleeves or trouser cuffs. Chain-gipsies have a predilection for such things, and lie in wait to grab at them.

● **Use of the echo sounder** There are two possibilities with this instrument:
(1) It has a cockpit repeater. Most convenient set-up, which allows the helmsman to keep an eye on the depth directly, as the boat enters the chosen area for anchoring.
(2) The apparatus is installed below, and has no repeater. In this case, a crew member must be designated whose sole job is to read out the soundings aloud every five or ten seconds, according to depth and other circumstances. A child can do this job perfectly.

If you have neither repeater nor a spare crew member, you will have to do the job yourself; at sea, the danger is the land. And it is imperative to know at every moment where it is. Especially when there is a risk of it rising up under your keel.

Left: never like this! Unbagged sp[i]naker, boom still rigged, barefoot crew, and the skipper is preparing anchor. . . .

Above: chain flaked down on the foredeck, to ensure that it pays ou[t] smoothly.

● Preparation of the cable

The foredeck hand first rem[oves] the safety lashings from the [main] anchor, and ensures that the[re is] nothing to prevent it from b[eing] dropped as soon as the ord[er is] given. If there is a windlass, he [will] have been provided with the [con]trol lever for the brake (o[ften] stowed with the handles [for the] halyard winches), and will c[heck] that the ratchet is in the vee[ring] position.

If there is no windlass, it ma[y be] advantageous to flake down [a few] fathoms or so of chain on [the] foredeck, and make it fast so [that] this length can be veered qu[ickly] once the anchor is let go. This [may] be particularly important if [the] cable is stowed without a ch[ain] pipe. It is also prudent, on la[rger] boats, to secure the anchor [by] taking the chain round the sam[son] post in a round turn just aft o[f the] anchor.

If the anchor has a habit of [get]ting up opposition at the mo[ment] when it is to be let go from [the] stemhead fitting, or if it canno[t be] placed there in readiness, it ca[n be] useful to let it hang down from [the] stemhead roller, retained by [the] chain – but look out for your p[aint]work.

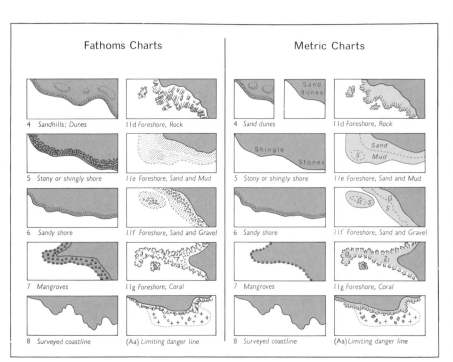

Fathoms Charts		Metric Charts	
4 Sandhills; Dunes	IId Foreshore, Rock	4 Sand dunes	IId Foreshore, Rock
5 Stony or shingly shore	IIe Foreshore, Sand and Mud	5 Stony or shingly shore	IIe Foreshore, Sand and Mud
6 Sandy shore	IIf Foreshore, Sand and Gravel	6 Sandy shore	IIf Foreshore, Sand and Gravel
7 Mangroves	IIg Foreshore, Coral	7 Mangroves	IIg Foreshore, Coral
8 Surveyed coastline	(Aa) Limiting danger line	8 Surveyed coastline	(Aa) Limiting danger line

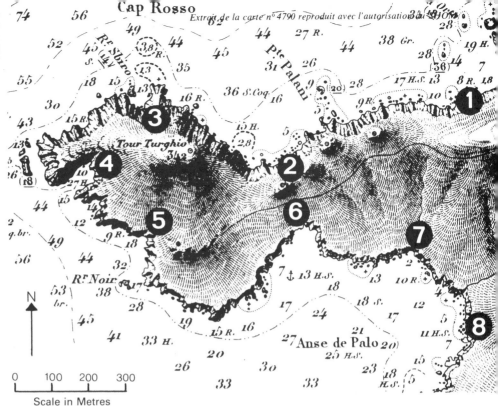

Cap Rosso

Extrait de la carte n° 4790 reproduit avec l'autorisation du SHOM

Tour Turghio

R⁺ Stirio

Pte Palani

R⁺ Noir

Anse de Palo

N

| 0 | 100 | 200 | 300 |

Scale in Metres

hoice of position to let go

t. Everything is ready forward, cleared, crew in position, echo nder running and anchor ready t go. In the cockpit, the skipper les the helmsman to bring the towards the shore, while keeping her away from the dangers ess he himself is carrying out function). Chart at the ready tidal situation memorised if ropriate, he will now decide the t of anchorage according to the wing factors:

- size and distribution of any waves
- protection from swell
- depth of water
- nature of the bottom
- length of the scope
- size of swinging circle
- presence of any reefs
- distance from the shore.

omplex group of factors which guide his choice within the rior of the chosen haven, and to ch we will have occasion to rn (notably as regards the th of scope and the size of the ging circle). The examples n here should give an idea of the analysis is made in a real ation. It nearly always has to be e quickly.

mple

time is nearly 1500, and in ember the days are short. It late morning when we left (Corsica) and Ajaccio is too far pe to get there before dark. So not show your crew what you

are capable of? One bit of luck for you: there is no tide in the Mediterranean. In this part there is no current either, and today there is no swell. Looking at the chart (above) there are eight anchorages available to your boat, which is 33 feet long and draws almost 5 feet. Try to make your choice for (1) a northerly, (2) a westerly, (3) a southerly and (4) an easterly wind. All of them moderate. . . .

Comments: the fact that there is neither tide nor current makes the study of the chart very much simpler. The soundings on the chart (shown in metres) will correspond in these waters pretty closely to the readings given by your echo sounder, and they will not change during the night. On the whole the shores are steep: there are a few clearly visible reefs, and only a dozen underwater rocks and one shoal to keep an eye on inshore. The following gives an idea of the rapid analysis a skipper would make, according to the different wind directions:

- **North wind.** Anchorages 1, 2, and 3, open to wind and swell, are no use. 4 is a possibility, but the southerly point of the creek forms a danger under the lee. Also, the enclosed position may produce gusts from any direction; only an anchorage for light winds. Number 5 is dangerous because of the threat to leeward (Rocher Noir), and the same applies to number 8. Numbers 6 and 7 remain, both good possibilities; my preference would be for number 6, which would be better sheltered if the wind backs westerly, always a probability in these waters.

- **West wind.** Only numbers 2 and 6 are possible, the latter being better protected from swell and less encumbered by rocks.

- **South wind.** Any of 1, 2 and 3 are practicable, number 2 offering the best swinging room, and the fewest problems in the event of a night departure.

- **East wind.** Possibilities, numbers 1, 4, 5, 7 and 8. The safest is certainly 8, with 4 the most picturesque.

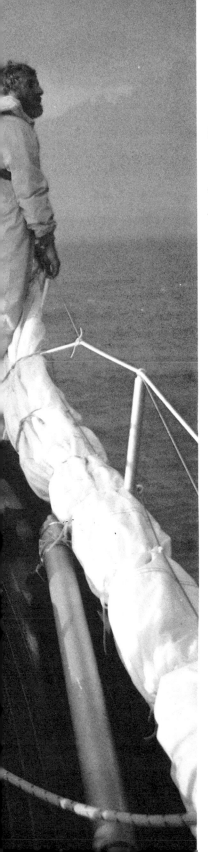

The manoeuvres of anchoring

Never be in a hurry. The arrival at an anchorage should be made slowly, to give plenty of time to sum up the situation. If the anchoring area is already encumbered by other boats, or if the skipper has the slightest doubt as to where best to let go to anchor, there should be no hesitation in making a preliminary tour of inspection to survey the soundings, distance from the shore, or proximity of downwind dangers.

This reconnaissance will in most cases avoid the necessity of hauling the anchor up again, having finished in a bad position. There is no reason for not making it, especially as we are manoeuvring under power, which is the assumption for this exercise. So now we have decided upon the exact point at which we want to come to rest. Now is the time to concentrate, as the success of the whole manoeuvre will depend upon the operations that follow.

Principal Operations

- decide on the scope
- approach head to wind
- stop the boat
- give the order to let go
- veer the cable
- make fast the cable
- verify that the anchor is holding
- check position
- note the course for departure.

Method of Dropping Anchor

(1) Decide on the scope, taking into account the depth of water. This length of cable veered is calculated as a function of the depth of water beneath the boat, and the wind strength. The tables given later in this chapter provide average values for all situations. They should only be taken as a *general* guide: the weight of the boat, nature of the bottom and amount of swell or sea will all have their influence on the holding of the anchor.

General rule: use three times the depth for depths over five fathoms, five times for shallower waters, even in good weather. And veer a little more if the needle of the anemometer looks like making an attempt on its altitude record.

(2) Approach at reduced speed for a distance roughly equal to the length of scope to be used; to achieve this it will be necessary to make use of marks on the shore.

(3) Stop the boat when this distance has been covered, then put the engine astern, keeping as nearly head to wind as possible.

Anchor over the bow, steering straig[ht] into the wind, the yacht advances at slow speed to the dropping position. Only when the boat begins to fall ba[ck] will the anchor be let go, and the cab[le] veered on demand.

A Wrong

The crewman [is] putting too gr[eat] braking force [on] the chain, and [the] anchor is dra[gged] along the bott[om] as the boat fa[lls] back, giving [no] chance to tak[e] hold.

B Wrong

Conversely, t[he] cable here ha[s] been veered t[oo] freely. The ch[ain] heaps itself u[p] in a pile on t[he] bottom, perh[aps on] top of the anc[hor.] Danger of fo[uling] or entanglem[ent.]

C Right

First, a length [of cable] equal to the d[epth] of water is ve[ered.] Then, when t[he] anchor is on [the] bottom, the r[est of] the cable is ve[ered] under control[, not] too freely, no[r too] meanly, until [the] desired scope [is] payed out.

(4) Give the order to let go as soon as the boat has stopped. The easiest way is to shout 'Let go!' to the foredeck hand, but he can also work from a hand signal (more discreet) or a short blast on a whistle. This should be agreed in advance. The important thing is that the anchor is let go at the correct moment, and that the cable is veered correctly: we shall see how later.

(5) Veer the cable, first to a length equal to the depth of water, then on demand: that is, under control and at the rate at which the boat is falling back. This control must be done with skill, to avoid:
— in case of too rapid paying out, the chain piling up in a heap on top of the anchor (risk of fouling) or on itself (risk of tangles);
— in case of too slow release, the anchor being dragged by the stern-way of the boat, as the short scope

so far released would tend to reduce the holding power of the anchor.

This control is done with a booted foot on small boats, or with the windlass brake in the case of boats so equipped (it takes some experience to appreciate the amount of braking power which is required). If a mixed cable is being used, the braking will be done manually once the length of chain is over the side, a round turn on the samson post or deck cleat allowing the rope to be stopped at any moment.

(6) Stop the release of cable when the previously arranged length of scope has been veered. The boat, motor in neutral, is then brought up sharply by the sudden tightening of the cable. Secure the cable firmly on the samson post, cleat or windlass (with the ratchet engaged), and wait for the boat to come head to wind.

Directions given by the skipper to the foredeck hand:

- put your boots on
- clear the foredeck
- remove anchor bolts and lashings
- place it ready to let go
- lay out the cable
- let go on the word of command
- veer freely a length of chain equal to the depth of water
- thereafter control the veering
- make fast the cable after veering the length of scope ordered.

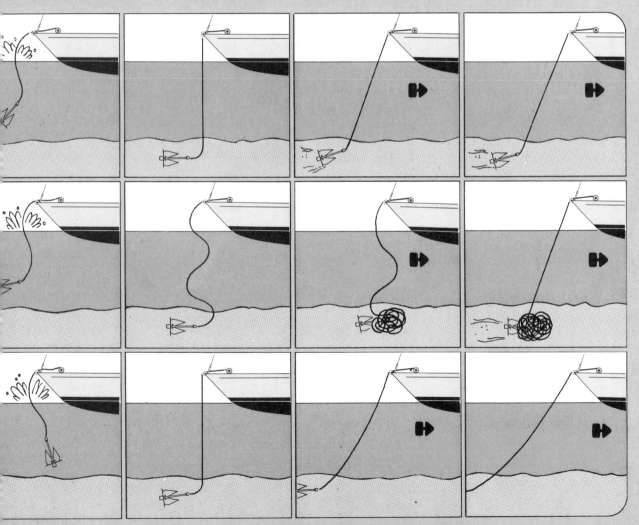

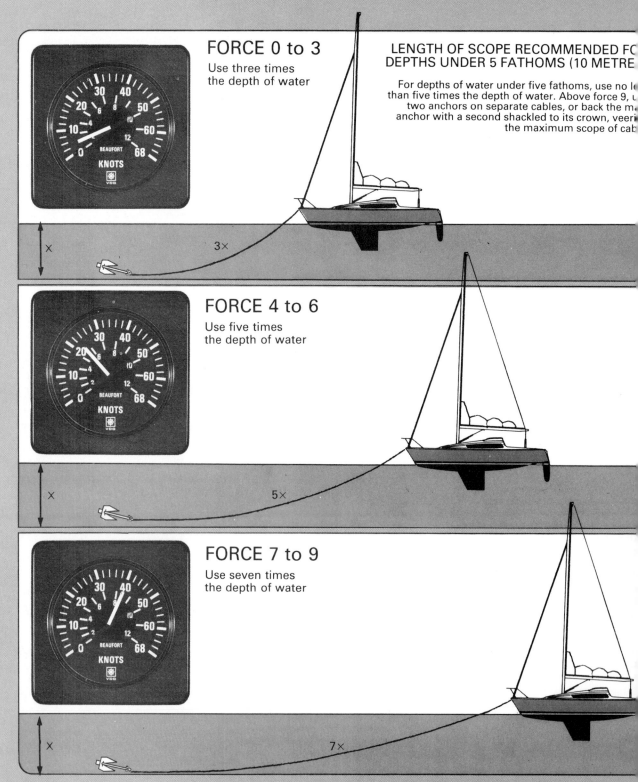

FORCE 0 to 3
Use three times
the depth of water

LENGTH OF SCOPE RECOMMENDED FO
DEPTHS UNDER 5 FATHOMS (10 METRE

For depths of water under five fathoms, use no le
than five times the depth of water. Above force 9, u
two anchors on separate cables, or back the m
anchor with a second shackled to its crown, veeri
the maximum scope of cab

$3\times$

X

FORCE 4 to 6
Use five times
the depth of water

$5\times$

X

FORCE 7 to 9
Use seven times
the depth of water

$7\times$

X

Before turning off the motor, check holding of the anchor by observing a transit between two fixed points [a]shore, in line and as far as possible [ap]art. Then make a note of the course [f]or leaving in case a night departure has to be made.

Check that the anchor is hold-[ing] by putting the motor astern [whi]le observing fixed objects [ab]eam. Only when confident that [the] anchor has a proper hold [sho]uld the motor be turned off.

Check the general situation at anchorage. The manoeuvre is [fini]shed, but there are still essential [pre]cautions to be taken to assure [the] safety of the boat.

Make sure that the range of the [tid]e does not require a modification [of] the decisions taken (length of [ro]pe, depth of water, currents).

Check the size of the swinging [circ]le, and make sure that there are [no] underwater hazards inside it, so [tha]t the boat will be kept off any [dan]gers even if the wind changes.

If bathing is part of the prog-[ra]mme after arrival, take advantage [of] this to dive and inspect the [nat]ure of the bottom and the posi-[tio]n of the anchor.

If not, use the hand lead to [bri]ng up a sample (we have seen [ho]w this is done). If it is mud or [we]ed, caution is indicated, and ex-[tra] chain should be veered or the [anc]hor doubled up, especially if the [bar]ometer is falling.

(9) Make a note of the course for leaving, so that the anchorage can be left in the dark in case of some nocturnal incident. They do happen: anchors that drag in a squall, a cable that parts as a result of an unexpected wave, a neighbouring boat swinging all over the available water when one cannot veer more line to keep out of the way because of dangers nearby – the examples are numerous. Always make a written note of the course to steer by compass if leaving at night after having weighed anchor (or sometimes even after leaving it to the fishes), while hoping that the note will never have to be used.

For my part, I have only used it once, but because of that I have never regretted taking the precaution. In 50 knots of wind, with three separate anchors out which refused to hold (this goes back to days when I still used unreliable anchors) and the buoy from a lobster pot caught round the propeller while manoeuvring in the pitch dark: the whole works! We shot out of there like a bullet, under a hastily hoisted jib, and nobody aboard saw a sign of a rock as we went. It was our only chance: having left our lines where they were, buoyed by a bunch of fenders there was nothing else we could do to avoid being driven ashore. The open sea really feels good after an escape like that!

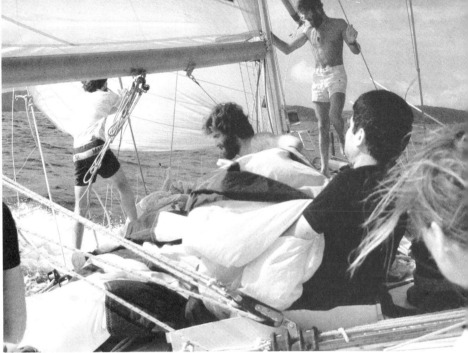

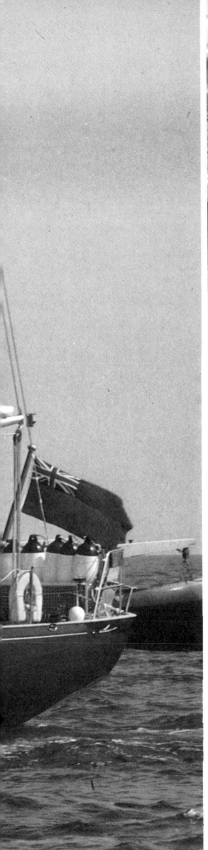

Arriving at the anchorage under sail, prudence demands a tour of inspection under a minimum of canvas.

ANCHORING UNDER SAIL

The technique of anchoring remains unchanged; the only problem is that the actual operations become rather more complicated than they are under power. The difficulties arise from the following main factors:

- restricted manoeuvrability
- multiplicity of operations
- reduced precision
- less immediate ability to check the holding

But although one should not begin until a solid base of experience has been acquired, after that one should take the chance of anchoring under sail whenever opportunity offers, for the love of the art of seamanship (not to be confused with showing off), and ultimately for security. Because you will be grateful for the practice if one day, in the middle of a crowded creek, your propeller refuses to obey orders, or even to discuss the matter.

Into the wind

The operation is similar to picking up a mooring. After a tour of reconnaissance under shortened sail, the final approach is made on a broad reach, or as near to that as possible, to preserve the greatest possible manoeuvrability. Ideally this should be under mainsail alone, as, if the jib has to be lowered at the last moment, this risks taking up the time of a hand, getting in the way on the foredeck, and putting the boat aback when she is brought up into the wind. So from every point of view it should be lowered as soon as possible.

Method (see sketch A on page 115): reaching across to the chosen position, at one or several boat-lengths from it, according to approach speed and windage (the stronger the wind, the less this distance will be), the jib is handed if this has not already been done, and the boat luffed sharply into the wind, hauling in the mainsheet in order to conserve maximum way. With the wind ahead, speed will fall off quickly as the sail flaps until the boat is stationary facing into the wind. At this moment the anchor should be let go.

Two methods of approaching an anchorage under sail:
* *Left, in light airs, approaching downwind; drop the mainsail first, and approach under jib, which is easier to lower, even if there is a sudden gust.*
* *Below, preparing to drop the mainsail.*

There are two possible ways of dealing with the mainsail:
* let it flap with eased sheet, to help the boat to fall back head to wind (mind your heads), or
* furl it as the anchor is let go, to avoid the sail filling if the boat's head falls off, or the boom causing an accident as it swings backwards and forwards across the deck.

The choice will depend on the strength of the wind (lower the sail if it is strong), space available and the tactical views of the skipper. Some prefer to keep the mainsail up until the operation of anchoring is successfully achieved, so that they can get under way again immediately if something goes wrong or the anchor fails to take hold (especially if there is no motor, or it cannot be used).

The remaining operations are identical to those set out in the last chapter, except that it will not be possible to check the holding of the anchor by putting the engine astern. But you can't have everything.

Downwind

A delicate and sometimes dangerous procedure, which demands the presence of a competent crew member on the foredeck, perfectly familiar with the gear concerned.

Advantage of anchoring downwind: the way on the boat, creating a sustained traction on the anchor cable, makes it easy to veer the cable and to check the holding of the anchor straight away.

Disadvantage: risk of damage to the hull by the cable before the boat has swung round head to wind, especially if she luffs in the opposite direction to the side of the chosen fairlead.

Method (see sketch B opposite): the approach to the chosen point is made under jib alone, so as to control the speed of the boat at around 1–2 knots, impossible under mainsail with a following wind. In strong winds, hand the jib

before reaching the anchoring position; in light airs keep it up until manoeuvre is finished.

A study of the sketch will scribe this operation far more simply than any words can. Remember above all that the cable must veered without interruption after the anchor has been let go, serious damage may be done to paintwork on the stem. Stop veering cable only at the moment when the helmsman puts the helm hard over to help the boat come head wind with the pull of the cable. Timing here is of the utmost importance.

WIND

*the boat stops:
let go!*

5

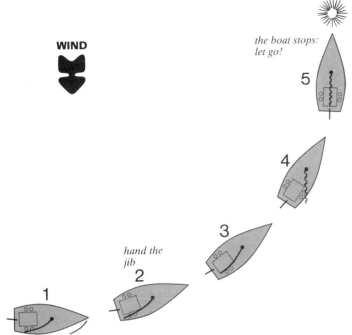

4

3

*hand the
jib*

2

1

a

Anchoring in a head wind.

(1) Sails set and drawing, the boat is steered towards the chosen point of anchorage in such a way as to arrive downwind of it.
(2) Begin to luff up towards it while handing the jib, so that the boat is being driven by mainsail alone.
(3) Continue the approach under mainsail, bringing the boat head to wind.
(4) Once head to wind, let the mainsheet fly. The boat loses way.
(5) When all way is off, let go the anchor and veer the cable under control as the boat falls back.

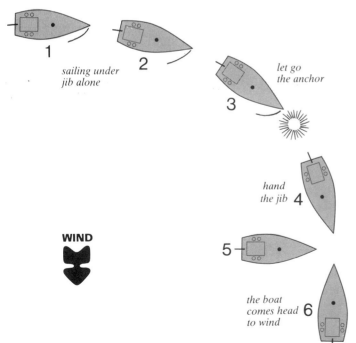

1

2

*sailing under
jib alone*

*let go
the anchor*

3

*hand
the jib* 4

WIND

5

*the boat
comes head* 6
to wind

b

Anchoring downwind

(1) Approach the point of anchorage under jib alone after furling the mainsail.
(2) In a stiff breeze (over force 5), hand the jib before anchoring. Otherwise, keep it set.
(3) Let go when the point of anchorage is reached, and veer the cable while the boat continues on course.
(4) If the jib has been left up, lower it when the boat has taken up all the scope of cable.
(5) As the cable tightens, and helped by the helmsman, the boat will be swung round head to wind. Check that the anchor is holding.

Left, a method of retrieving an anchor which has fouled a ground chain, and which has not been buoyed. (1), with cable hard up-and-down, lower a loop of chain down rode and shank, onto the crown. (2), slacken the cable, move boat forwards and pull anchor out backwards.

TO BUOY OR NOT TO BUOY?

That is the question. I can no longer count how many times, while getting under way, the whirring of the windlass has slowed alarmingly after three quarters of the cable has already returned peacefully to the comfort of the chain locker. Chain straight up and down, bows half submerged, cable rigid with tension until somebody says 'Someone is going to break something somewhere!' It doesn't take a professor to diagnose what is wrong: the anchor is fouled. All we have to find out is on what. Half the time it is only necessary to veer a bit of cable, then go forward a bit, to free the imprisoned flukes by changing the direction of the shank. If this fails, you can lower a loop of chain as shown in the illustration above, or put on a mask and dive to the bottom to see what is going on. *Pitcairn* always has a full diving bottle for this eventuality, and it has never yet been left alone for long enough to get rusty.

How do you avoid such an incident? When anchoring, use a tripping line attached to the crown of the anchor (turn back to page 78 to remind yourself of the characteristics of this bit of gear). This precaution usually worked when I used it over about ten years, during a period when diving equipment was little known, and boats were less numerous. Nowadays, the crowding of anchorages has reached such a level that the use of the tripping line has almost disappeared; partly in the search for simplicity, perhaps (the setting of a tripping line still has to be done by hand), and also to avoid its buoy acting as a trap for passing propellers. Set an anchor buoy above your anchor in a Corsican creek in August, and listen to the complaints from the dinghy drivers as they come back after dinner ashore! It is enough to discourage the most intrepid.

No, as I have said, the use of a tripping line can only be considered nowadays in winter, and in areas not used by board-sailors. Unless it is submerged, which complicates the process and partly reduces its efficiency, the most rational solution is to bring the end of the tripping line back aboard, or to attach it to the chain just below the surface. The sketches opposite show the advantages and disadvantages of each method. In practice, it would seem that the tripping line is now only used in exceptional circumstances, and that is probably how best to regard it, even if some elderly enthusiast in your crew, covered in commemorative medals, tells you otherwise.

1

Tripping line brought back aboard

The most practical solution.

Advantages: Ease of adjustm[ent] from the boat, immediate availa[bil]ity in case of need, no buoy or[?] below the surface.

Disadvantages: Necessity of sim[ul]taneous adjustment with anchor chain, on pain of finding [the] boat swinging to the tripping lin[e if] cable is veered without lengthen[ing] it as well; risk of entangling the l[ine] with the cable.

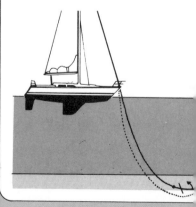

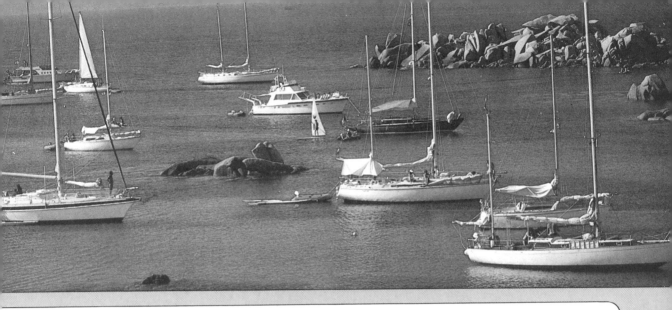

2	**3**	**4**
### Tripping line attached to the anchor cable	### Tripping line attached to a surface buoy	### Tripping line attached to a submerged buoy

...not should be made just be-... ...e surface.

...ntages: Ability to veer more ... without bothering about the ...ng line; no buoy.

...vantages: As in alternative 1, ...t for the first.

Advantages: Position directly above the anchor, allowing its location to be seen at all times; ease of recovery of the anchor if it is fouled; no risk of entanglement with cable.

Disadvantages: Risk of fouling the propellers of boats or dinghies passing nearby, or of bumping against the hull while swinging at night.

The buoy should be below the level of propellers, and if possible of keels.

Advantages: No risk of catching propellers, or of entanglement with cable.

Disadvantages: Difficulty of recovery, especially at high water in tidal ports; need to use the dinghy if the anchor is fouled.

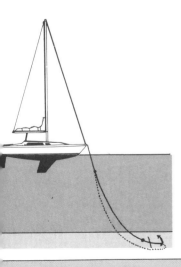

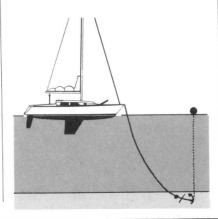

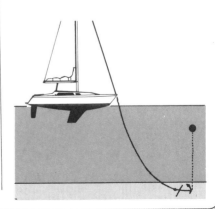

Rme de Biri   Manica   Sabia
Rme

B. de Walwich   DAMARAS   BETJOUANAS
Cuivre
G. S. Thomas   Montagnes   R. Inhamb
Fich   Garroumana R.   Mocica   Inhaqua Fort
GRANDS NAMAQUOIS   Zitakou   Lagoino
Namaquois   Orange Fe   TAMBOUKIS   GONIQUOIS
C. Voltas   PETITS NAMAQUOIS   Côte de Natal
Dest. de Karrou
B. S. Helene   Nieuweld M.   Graaf Reynet
COLONIE HOLLANDAISE
B. de la Table   Zwarte Berg M.   Camdebou
Ville du Cap   R. des Elephans   R. Dimanche
C. de B. Esperance   de Plettenberg
False Bay   Ks. d. Mossel
Falso   C. des Aiguilles

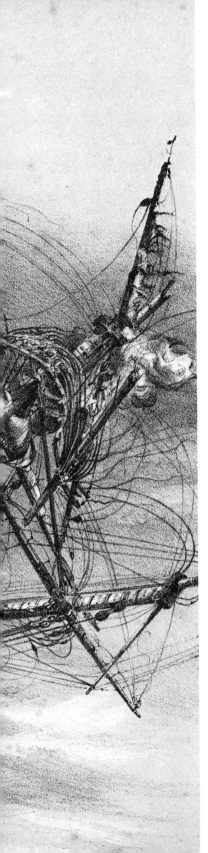

Anchoring in strong winds

Unless you have chosen a site where there are violent currents, or which suffers the effects of an unforeseen tide, anchoring accidents rarely happen in good weather. The real problems begin when the wind increases, as the windage of the boat and the state of the sea have a direct effect on the holding of our anchors.

Although as far as actual anchoring is concerned the broad lines of technique remain unchanged, there are some additional actions we can take to increase the security of a boat at anchor. The choice of these will mainly be determined by:

- the intensity of the gusts
- the sea conditions
- the immediate environment
- the characteristics of the tide
- the equipment available.

The following extract from *A Treatise on Manoeuvres* by Bonnefoux, published at the beginning of the 19th century, contains a remarkable example of the benefits of lengthening the scope in bad weather.

'In Table Bay in 1805, during one of those gales which gave the Cape of Good Hope the name of Cape of Storms, the French frigate Belle Poule suffered the successive parting of all of the several cables to which she was lying. There seemed no hope but to beach the vessel on one of the less rocky shores of this haven, upon which two English vessels had shortly before been lost with crew and cargo. The order to hoist the storm jib was given, when the lieutenant of the watch, who had a heavy emergency anchor ready, thought of it and proposed that it should be tried. The hoisting of the jib was stopped and the anchor was let go, a second hawser was quickly added to the first, and on these slender ropes, which together made a scope of two hundred and forty fathoms, the frigate held and was saved. Almost immediately, the same misfortune befell another frigate, but the emergency anchor was not ready for use, and she was driven ashore.'

I

Lengthen the scope

This is the first thing to do if the swinging circle will permit. By veering extra cable, the pull on the shank will become more horizontal, which will have the effect of increasing its penetration into the bottom, especially if the cable is all chain.

Advantages:
- improved holding of the anchor
- reduced snubbing
- greater elasticity of the line.

Disadvantages:
- increased swinging circle
- longer cable to recover
- in deep water, it will require a substantial length of cable.

The exercise of lengthening the scope of cable, by causing an extension of the swinging circle, can often produce problems where the anchorage is confined or crowded.

Influence of length of scope on swinging circle

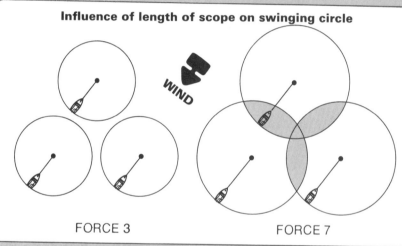

FORCE 3   FORCE 7

If, in rising wind, it is necessary to increase the scope, the swinging circles are increased by a similar amount. When the boats are close together, this should cause no immediate problems as long as the cables are veered simultaneously. Below, the leeward boat may have difficulty in weighing anchor.

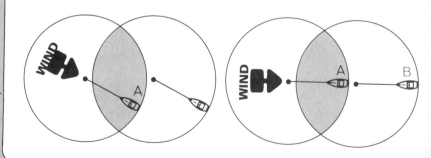

...pretty well impossible to put down two anchors side by side using sail alone, especially if the boat is already lying to one anchor, as here. Two possible solutions: use the motor, or carry the second anchor to its position in the tender.

Mooring with two anchors: the fork moor

...oring (a boat lying to one ...chor is *anchored*; lying to two ... is *moored*) to two anchors ...ead at an angle is a common ...thod. The second anchor is ...pped the same distance ahead ...the boat as the first, so that an ...gle of between 30° and 120° is ...med by the two cables. The boat ...moored correctly when the strain ...posed by wind and sea is divided ...ually between the two cables.

...vantages:
...reinforcement of the holding ...power
...limitation of swinging circle
...reduction of yawing
...simplicity
...increased security owing to the presence of two independent cables, separately anchored and belayed.

...sadvantages:
...need to row the second anchor ...to position in the tender in boats ...thout motor

● risk of twisting the cables around each other.

Principle

The second anchor should be dropped at a distance from the first, calculated so that the angle between the two cables when they are tight is:
− between 30° and 120° in calm weather
− less than 45° in strong winds.

The angle achieved is a function of the distance between the anchors and the length of scope: if the second anchor is dropped the length of the scope from the first, the angle will be 60°, as the two anchors and the stem of the boat will form an isosceles triangle. This is a reasonable moor, which I personally use almost always for added security when in open anchorages — frequently, in other words.

If the wind increases, then if circumstances permit (and if they do not you should not have chosen the anchorage) it is enough to lengthen each cable by a few fathoms to

decrease the angle of the fork, which has the advantage of preserving an equal load between the two anchors, while reducing the total strain by diminishing the sideways component of the pull.

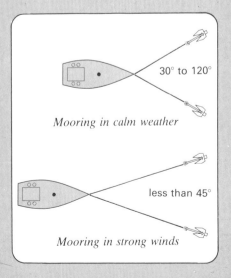

Mooring in calm weather

30° to 120°

less than 45°

Mooring in strong winds

Laying second anchor using motor

start up!   *full ahead!*   *let go!*   *the final result*

Laying second anchor using tender

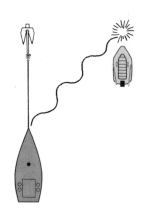

lying to main anchor   *tender makes to windward*   *second anchor is dropped*   *the final result*

Method

● **On arrival** at the anchorage under power, it is perfectly simple to lay two anchors in a single operation. The best method for ease of handling is to lay the anchor with mixed cable first, and veer this on demand until the position has been reached for the main anchor to be let go. The scopes are then adjusted to the required length under tension as the boat comes head to wind and falls back.

● **After arrival.** When already lying to the main anchor, steer upwind and to one side of the line of the first cable, paying it out freely. When in position, let go the second anchor, and adjust both cables as the boat falls back.

If there is no motor, it is no use trying to lay a second anchor under sail: this is impossible. The operation must be carried out with the aid of the tender, preferably equipped with an outboard if the water is choppy (see sketch). The anchor may be carried in the bottom of the

dinghy, or hooked on the st▢ ready to drop. The length of c▢ should all be piled in the dingh▢ that only rope is being pulled f▢ the boat's foredeck: otherwise▢ weight of the chain will impede▢ progress. It is important to v▢ quickly, as wind and current pu▢ a heavy resistance to progres▢ the breeze is stiff; a hesitatio▢ only a few seconds before let▢ go the anchor will soon dem▢ trate the speed at which an in▢ able dinghy is capable of driftin▢ a thirty knot gust!

Picture of a two-anchor moor taken from France Maritime of 1835, which should make us think twice before complaining about the weight of our warps.

ollowing extract from an
e by marine architect Henri
n, was printed in 'Le Yacht',
June 1935.

*an anchored vessel must still be
dered subject to the hazards of
at sea, it is virtually never suf-
to lie to only one anchor. On
ccasion one may need to lay a
d, perhaps because bad weather
s doubt on the holding of a single
r, perhaps because the radius of
nging circle needs to be reduced.
latter case the angle between the
s should be between 60° and 120°,
e length of each scope should be
hat – as far as the depth of water
its – there is no risk of fouling, or
boat being damaged by the upper
of one of its anchors at low water.
therefore prudent to carry two
rs aboard. When this need to lay
nchors arises, care must be taken
he movements of the vessel due to
streams and gusts do not result in
ouling of one of the anchors. If
is no need to reduce the swinging
, the angle between the two cables
d be no more than 15° or 20°.'*

e should note that only
erman-type anchors or models
massive crowns were in use
g the period when this extract
written. Thanks to the superior
ing power of modern anchors,
ast figure mentioned can now
ncreased to 40° or 45°.

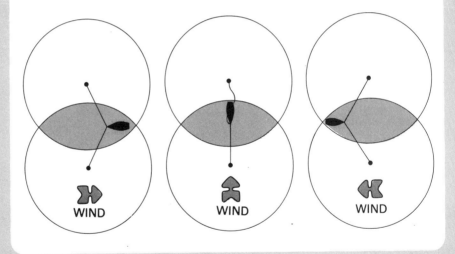

With two anchors, the area covered when swinging is reduced

WIND   WIND   WIND

In the last century, a ship's boat was used to carry out a kedge to windward of the ship to achieve a two-anchor moor. This anchor was solidly secured to the stern of the boat, and dropped with its tripping line.

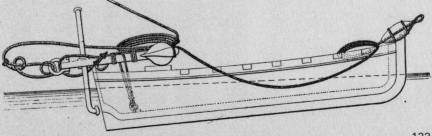

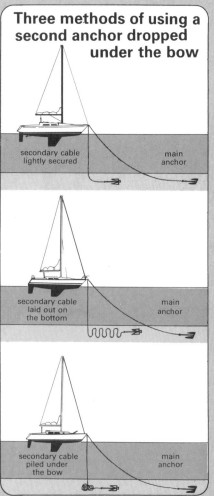

Three methods of using a second anchor dropped under the bow

secondary cable
lightly secured

main
anchor

secondary cable
laid out on
the bottom

main
anchor

secondary cable
piled under
the bow

main
anchor

3

Dropping an anchor under the bow

The use of this method was once very popular on large sailing vessels because of their inability to lay two anchors for a fork moor, and the great weight of the anchors which made them difficult to carry in a ship's boat; however, it has now almost disappeared with the arrival of auxiliary motors.

Principle: a vessel lying to one anchor and afraid that it might drag would drop a second straight under the bow, taking advantage of a fairlead on the opposite side to that already in use. The length of chain veered was kept to a minimum, to avoid fouling the anchor, and the chain pawl was left disengaged. As soon as the main anchor began to drag, the second chain would begin to run out noisily, warning the crew. It would then be progressively braked, until the vessel was lying to doubled anchors, i.e. one in front of the other on separate cables, ready to face the gale.

One method dear to the e͏ teachers at the famous French s͏ ing school at Glénans – perha͏ is still used in the archipelag͏ consisted of falling back a͏ metres after dropping the ke͏ and then throwing out the whol͏ the chain in a pile below the b͏ Using this technique, the͏ stretches itself along the botto͏ the main anchor drags, without͏ intervention being needed. Ad͏ tages of the method: no risk͏ fouling the anchor, and no need͏ surveillance.

I have personally never͏ perimented with this method,͏ the proximity of the two cables͏ the bottom does not seem to m͏ assure perfect holding for the͏ anchor. We shall see why.

In the photo on the right the second cable of an anchor dropped under bow to reinforce the main one in c͏ of dragging or accidental breakage be clearly seen. One would still pre͏ the proper two-anchor fork moorin͏ when the swinging area is restricted

...graving by Romargue illustrating a ...noeuvre carried out with the aid of ...Santa Maria's boat. The treatment ...the scene suggests that the ship was ...aground on a shoal: otherwise how ...would the boat have succeeded in ...rtaking the ship in spite of the speed ...given her by her bellying foresail?

4

Doubled anchors

The following is an extract from *The Sailor's Manual*, drawn up in 1950 by Captain R. de Parfouru:

'*One may lie to doubled anchors when, arriving at an anchorage in bad weather, there is fear that the main anchor may drag and allow the vessel to be driven ashore. In this case the two anchors are dropped from the cathead simultaneously or at very short intervals. The cables pay out in the same direction, and care must be taken to adjust them so that each of them is bearing one half of the strain.*'

The author (who, be it said in passing, merely copied word for word a passage from the *Seamanship Manual* of the Naval School, published in 1891) states that this type of moor is excellent for resisting a gale, while always remembering the risk of fouling one of the anchors. That is why this method is only mentioned for historic interest, as its use in practice is hardly justified on yachts. The fork moor, or even better in really heavy weather, the backing of the main anchor (which will be described shortly), will always produce better results. All the same, if one of the anchors of a fork moor drags, a doubled anchor moor will accidentally result. My personal advice is not to allow this situation to remain for too long, to avoid the twisting together of the cables as a result of changes of heading caused by variations in wind and current.

Doubled anchor moor. The situation can also occur as the result of a fork moor, one of whose anchors has dragged.

5

Backing an anchor

Backing an anchor is without any doubt the method which produces the greatest holding power from the anchors in question in strong winds. All experienced sailors are unanimous on this, even though they may deplore the difficulties of putting it into effect belatedly.

Principle: The main anchor is backed by attaching a secondary anchor to its crown by a short length of chain. This backwards pull holds down the main anchor against the bottom, and increases its holding power by a substantial amount.

Advantages: This method of reinforcing the holding does not require a second anchor cable, thus freeing the hawser that would be needed for other uses (a line taken ashore or to a buoy to hold the boat, keeping her off a danger or limiting the swinging area). In addition, it derives great efficiency from a second anchor of light weight, accompanied by a length of chain only a couple of fathoms long. This can be of life-saving importance in a badly equipped boat, or where an anchor has been intentionally or accidentally abandoned.

Disadvantages: There are four.

● The swinging circle remains unreduced, in contrast to the fork moor.

● All the pressure from wind and waves falls upon a single cable, with all the risks that that entails in the event of failure of one of its elements.

● The backing of the anchor must be carried out before the arrival of the gale, as otherwise grave difficulties may be encountered in carrying out the manoeuvre.

● The additional weight may cause problems in weighing anchor to get under way.

Installation: The anchor used for backing need only be of half the weight of the anchor to be backed.

For a 26 foot boat normally usi 26 lb anchor, an 11–18 lb mode serve perfectly. The chain benefit from a similar reduct its calibre need only correspon the weight of the backing an and no more (see table on p 33).

The length of the chain joi the two anchors may reasonabl from one to two fathoms. S people say that only a foot or needed, but for my part I thi greater length is required to the backing anchor behind the row cut by the main anchor v digging in, especially with soft toms: mud, some sands or debris.

If no chain is available, it ca replaced by nylon rope. But this one disadvantage, as well as danger of chafe from certain ty of bottom: its elasticity may vent the two anchors from wor together, which is vital if the quired efficiency is to be obtai

Note that it is not necessar use two anchors of the same The first can be a CQR and second of the Danforth type. important thing is to be abl shackle the chain of the bac anchor onto the crown of the r anchor. Most anchors have a or a hole for this purpose, allo the use of a shackle or a snap-h

...acking anchor attached by ...of a doubled chain. Any lin- ...ill do, as long as the two ...rs work simultaneously. It is ...ant to prepare the equipment in ...e, so as not to have to haul out ...er end of the main cable to cut ...necessary length of chain in an ...ncy!

...heavy things, anchors. So you ...agine what two feel like. . . .

...od: Backing an anchor is an ...tion which is normally used ...the wind has reached an ...al level, and when a fork ...has proved insufficient. It is ...ore almost always carried out ...emergency measure: all the ...reason to practise first in ...weather.

...re are two possibilities:

...king the anchor on arrival. ...s the easiest method. The two ...rs are joined while on the ...ck, and let go together in the ...al way. Advantages: speed of ..., anchor able to support a ...quent rise in the wind, avoi- ...of the need to work later in ...weather. Disadvantage: grea- ...veight to haul up when ...ing. I know some skippers ...try to reduce this snag by ...hening the joining chain until ...nger than the depth of water. ...g up the anchors separately, ...claim in this way to have ...ed the increase in weight ...d by backing the anchor. But ...be serious: five fathoms of ...of appropriate calibre is al- ...heavier than the anchor that ...e attached to it, so where is ...aving?

...instance, a 10 kg anchor ...res a chain of 8 mm ($^5/_{16}$") ...ing 1.50 kg/metre, so 15 kg

anchors attached directly
one to the other

anchors joined by one to two fathoms of chain

Armand Colin, inventor of the Britany models, recommend fixing the shank of the backing anchor directly to the crown of the bower. Personally, I prefer to avoid the furrow of the main anchor by interposing a length of chain between the two.

In heavy weather, the junctions between the different elements of the cable are subjected to massive strain. It is therefore vital to check them carefully before use, tightening shackles with pliers and securing them with stainless steel wire.

for ten metres, while a 16 kg model will need a 9.5 mm chain weighing 2.35 kg/metre and thus 23½ kilos for ten metres: an easy calculation which shows that the longer chain option provides a false solution to the weight problem. As for the use of a long rope to join the anchors with the same purpose, its elasticity will risk reducing the efficiency of the backing anchor.

● **Backing when already anchored.** Only one solution: haul up the main anchor to fix the backing anchor to its crown. A tripping line facilitates this manoeuvre; during a lull, the boat is held by the use of the motor or by trying to get a temporary grip with a second anchor (perhaps one of a fork moor that has dragged), then the main anchor is hauled up from the dinghy by the tripping line. In five seconds (six if it is dark...) the backing anchor is attached and the two returned to the bottom, with a minimum of fatigue. Without the tripping line the whole anchor and chain has to be recovered to do the job, a task that seldom adds to the joy of life.

In conclusion, backing the anchor is normally only a resort for very bad weather (winds over 45 knots). The fork moor is usually enough to cope with lesser winds.

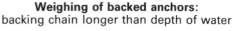

Weighing of backed anchors:
backing chain longer than depth of water

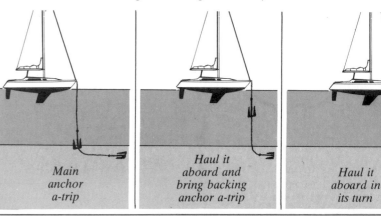

Main anchor a-trip

Haul it aboard and bring backing anchor a-trip

Haul it aboard in its turn

Weighing of backed anchors:
backing chain short, but tripping line on second anchor

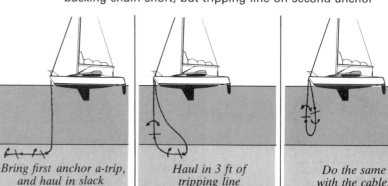

Bring first anchor a-trip, and haul in slack of tripping line

Haul in 3 ft of tripping line and belay

Do the same with the cable, and so on

6

Shore lines

Although hardly ever mentioned in technical works, this method offers the best guarantee of holding when the wind is blowing violently from a steady direction. I remember a series of force 9–10 squalls which rocked us to sleep in every one of our anchorages on the occasion of a cruise along the Turkish coast which was marked by an incessant *meltemi*, which sometimes happens in those waters during August. With only two of us aboard, our hours of sleep were so precious that Monique and I did not recover until we took to making a heavy 22 mm hawser fast to a rock upwind: one weighing several tons, and preferably of granite. The wind direction having never varied by one degree in three weeks, this solution proved totally efficient as a complement to the normal use of anchors.

Lateral land-lines are sometimes necessary in narrow creeks.

We will see later how it is possible to use warps to limit the swinging area, for instance when the anchorage is too narrow or too crowded to allow the boat to swing freely round her anchor. Even when the wind or current holds her in a constant direction, a land-line made fast to a rock or tree will reduce the strain on the anchor (by reducing yawing), and also on the skipper in a stiff breeze. She can be held head or stern to wind, as in this photograph of Pitcairn *at Minorca.*

Method of use

Land-lines can be used in the lee of any kind of shore, on condition that the direction of the gusts does not vary. It is wise to put a kedge anchor out in the opposite direction, from the bow or stern according to the situation, leaving enough slack on its cable to give the boat some freedom to swing.

Warps taken ashore can also limit the swinging area or even totally immobilise a boat in a narrow anchorage. If buoyant polypropylene is chosen, they offer so little resistance as they float that they can easily be towed ashore in the dinghy, or even by a swimmer. But remember to mark them by means of fenders if there is a risk of another boat fouling them.

To sum up, one may conclude that of all the procedures available to us for reinforcing the holding of an anchor, the fork moor is generally the most convenient, while backing the anchor gives the greatest security in really heavy weather, getting it done as early as possible in the proceedings.

Admittedly, no method will allow an anchor to get a hold on a rocky plateau, or prevent defective or too weak material from failing under the strain. As far as anchorages are concerned, special cases are numerous and the tactics to adopt depend on a set of infinitely variable parameters. It is up to every skipper to satisfy himself as to the quality of the equipment aboard, and to decide in view of the circumstances of the moment which technique to use to assure the security of his boat – which is, after all, no more than the definition of his duty at all times at sea.

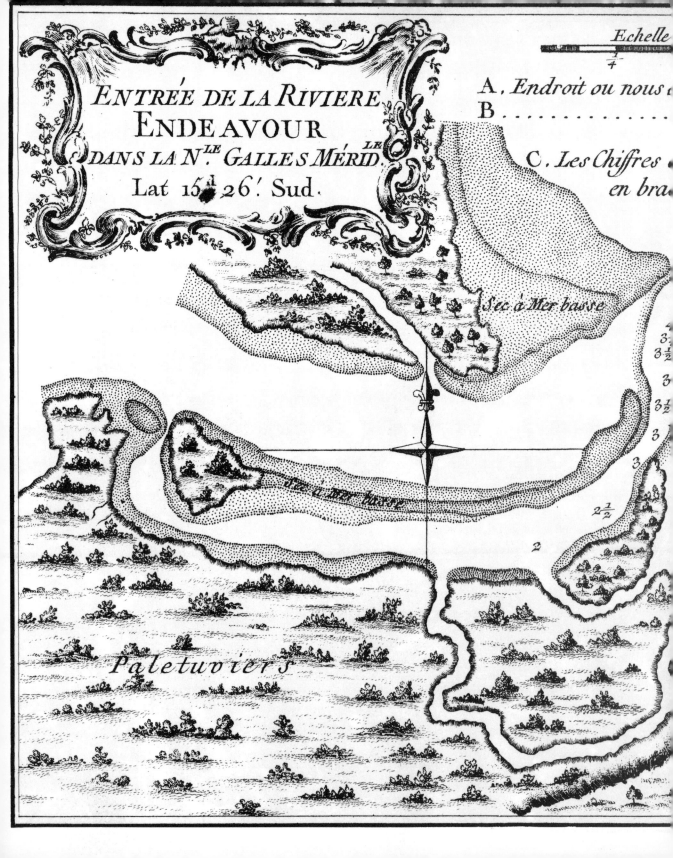

ENTRÉE DE LA RIVIERE
ENDEAVOUR
DANS LA N.LE GALLES MÉRID.LE
Lat 15 26' Sud.

Echelle

A. Endroit ou nous
B. . . . .

C. Les Chiffres
en bra

Sec à Mer basse

Sec à Mer basse

Paletuviers

$\frac{3}{4}$

$3\frac{1}{2}$

3

$3\frac{1}{2}$

3

3

$2\frac{1}{2}$

2

es notre equippement.
es le Vaisseau.

profondeur de l'eau
Mer basse.

4   4½   5
3

Special cases

Emergency Anchorage

Exceptional circumstances can arise in which a boat suffers an accident while under way which compels her to anchor as rapidly as possible. Exceptional, but alas more frequent than inexperienced people might think. Leaving l'Aberwrac'h in 1977 in a nor'wester of force 4 or 5, I was engaged in hanking on the heavy genoa while Monique steered *Pitcairn* out by the channel, straight into the wind, when, just as I was ready to hoist the sail, the Perkins coughed, and then died. We had just passed the Grand Pot de Beurre beacon tower. The shoals of Libenter showed their formidable teeth fifty yards to leeward, and just as I was hoisting the genoa I saw that the halyard was the wrong side of a spreader. No use thinking that in five seconds I could haul down the sail, change to a spinnaker halyard and rehoist it, or hoping that we could sail our way out almost straight into the wind under mainsail alone. Even as I thought about it, the rocks had got twenty yards nearer to the stern. Undoing the lashing and throwing the CQR from the stemhead was accomplished at the speed of lightning. When the boat came to rest at the end of a cable which had been kept to the minimum reasonable length, a shrimp would have had a

job to squeeze between our transom and the first of the reefs, which were foaming with rage.

I have the same memory coloured by the sun of Antigua, of Naples, of a list of sites as long as a three-volume dictionary, resulting from the parting of a rudder-chain, the failure of a tiller retaining pin, and a jib caught aback after a tumultuous attempt to tack in a narrow channel.

The presence of the tender on tow adds an appreciable safety factor if boat is overtaken by bad weather while approaching the coast. It can brought into instant action to lay on an anchor in the case of failure of rigging or engine – which has often happened to me.

The occasions when the anchor can be needed in a hurry are numerous enough to make it essential for it always to be instantly available. Not with an anchor on the stemhead and the cable in a locker or the other way round; it is vital at all times that one should be able to anchor in a few seconds, without the least delay. The excuse, after an accident, that 'It was impossible to get a warp onto the anchor in such a short time' underlines a grave fault, which one can qualify as inadmissible. Bearing in mind that at sea the real danger always comes from the land, I would suggest that this precaution should be the first rule on any cruising boat. Reading the stories of Erling Tambs and Jean Lacombe printed elsewhere in this book can only confirm us in this belief.

Method: Imperative number one is speed of execution. Unless the anchor and gear are all laid out and ready to let go, this requires the speedy intervention of a crew member who knows the gear. Therefore never cast off from a quay without having shown one of the crew how to operate it, in case the need arises while rounding the pierhead. Especially if you are leaving under power. You will not be the first to whom this has happened: trailing ropes to catch propellers, or plastic bags blocking cooling water intakes are always common around harbours.

It seems to me important to consider in advance the possibility of anchoring in such circumstances. Most skippers, when some accident happens upwind of a danger, immediately think of trying to escape by the dynamic means that are available: using the engine if the failure is of sail, using the sail if it is the engine that has let them down. An honourable reflex, but with the disadvantage (especially in the case of making sail) of imposing a certain delay, and thus increasing the risk of grounding. And ringing the engine full steam ahead will not produce the required effect if a rope's end gets caught up in the propeller.

And don't tell me that would be too much of a coincidence! I know from experience that one accident almost always brings another in its wake, simply because everything is being done in a hurry, if not in a panic. The wind gets up; the genoa is lowered and falls into the water. One of the crew tries to rescue it, and slips into the sea. The helmsman decides to start the motor to help in picking him up; the genoa sheet, untended, goes over the side and winds itself round the shaft, immobilising the boat. Tragic, but unfortunately also classic!

When there is a danger to lee-ward and it seems that the b may quickly be carried down o it, make up your mind while there still time: anchor. It is rare coasts to be so steep-to that c will not find bottom twenty met from a reef or the base of a je Anchor without delay, using th to five times the depth of wa shown by the sounder (assum you have time to use it) and tak account of the distance off danger. If the motor is operati start it and lower sail at once reduce windage. When the b comes head to wind, reduce violent strain on the anchor caus by the effort of stopping the drift boat by going ahead on the engi Even in very strong wind, anc and propeller together will hold boat out of danger until there been time to repair the damage. is the motor that has failed, greatest possible length of ca must be veered, and a seco anchor got ready to reinforce first in case of squalls or stro current.

Final eventuality: the anc does not take hold; the motor fuses all co-operation and sail c not be set. It is time to think ab putting up the values on your in ance policy, because whatever y try to do, you have little chance avoiding an almost certain ca trophe. As I have said, dangers leeward mean maximum risk.

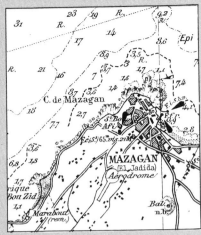

Photograph of Hippocampe (Sea-horse) from the book by Jean Lacombe published in 1957. Note in passing the topping lift, no doubt tense with the emotion of departure. . . .

'I have hardly got to sleep when I think I hear a scraping noise. Again. The whole boat vibrates. No doubt about it, my keel is touching. I leap into the cockpit. I can see nothing, because some of the fog has returned. I can only hear the sea slapping against the shore.

'Impossible to sail, there is no wind. What can I do? Anchor? The anchor is buried in the forepeak; impossible to get it out. This is the trouble with very small boats. I used the little forepeak to stow my anchor, some jerrycans of water and the inflatable dinghy. Every one of these should be ready to grab at need, but obviously it was impossible for everything to be stowed on top. Unfortunately, at this moment it was the anchor I needed that was underneath.

'The keel struck more violently. The boat swung round to port and, pushed by the waves, grounded beam on.'

Happily, the boat was saved, thanks to favourable weather, which allowed us to share a pleasure; the ingenuous Jean Lacombe's book would not otherwise have been published, which would have been a pity. (From *The Atlantic is Mine* by Jean Lacombe; Robert Laffont, 1957.)

coastal sailing, that is to say, en within fifty miles of the rest land, it is vital to be able to chor instantly. Not in a minute, even thirty seconds; the anchor uld fall from the bow like light- g. Which means that anchor and le must be kept ready at all es, so that it takes only a fraction a second to free it in the hope of ping the boat off unexpected gers to lee. It happens more en than some people think. Jean combe learned that to his cost ring his first months of ocean ising.

'Saturday 16th July.
'No. The land didn't want to play. Yesterday evening was foggy. I ran along the coast without seeing it. . . . At nine o'clock, the fog clearing, I saw a light, quite close. One great white flash every five seconds. Quick, the List of Lights. My electric lamp has dimmed, I can hardly read it. Here it is: it must be Sidi Bou Afi at Mazagan.

'It is almost straight overhead: clearly I can't be far out to sea. But I can't hear the breakers on the coast, so that is all right. Completely becalmed, there is nothing I can do; I lower sail and turn in.

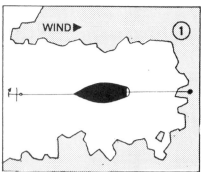

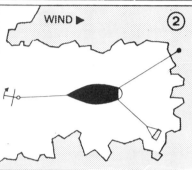

These two sketches illustrate two methods of securing a boat when lack of room in the anchorage will not permit of her swinging freely. In this situation, it is important to secure bow to the open sea, in case need arises to get out in a hurry. In the photograph, Pitcairn lies to quarter ropes in the clear waters of a Minorcan creek. A jewel-box made in paradise.

Control of swinging by the use of warps

Seldom mentioned in the textbooks, this technique is of value because it allows shelter to be taken in narrow creeks and bays, which tend to be the more peaceful because there is only room for one boat. I need hardly say that these are the favourite kinds of anchorage for lovers of quiet, as I am. Having done it often, I think I am pretty well up in the technique.

Principle: When the boat is lying to her anchor facing out to sea, she is held in position by warps from her stern.

Advantage: The ability to make use of small indentations in the coast, far from the bustle of the crowded bays.

Disadvantages: A technique to be used only in very good weather, or if it is certain that the established wind will not change. Need to moor facing the open for safety if a rapid departure becomes necessary. This involves stern to wind if it is blowing offshore, or bow exposed to the sea in the contrary case, for which reason this solution will only be used if the forecast is good.

Technique: The sketches and photographs speak for themselves. As every situation demands a special mooring, it is difficult to provide any universally valid hints. According to the location, it may be an idea to take the warps ashore first in the dinghy and secure them temporarily, only then manoeuvring the boat into the creek, falling back onto the ropes after anchoring. Secure the warps to trees or around large rocks, taking care in tidal areas that the knots will not be covered at high water, which will complicate their release when leaving, unless they are passed round and returned aboard.

The use of buoyant polypropylene rope (see page 77) will undoubtedly make the business of getting the lines ashore easier. Mooring with land-lines displays its greatest value in the Mediterranean and other relatively tideless waters: a substantial tidal range (or indeed a heavy swell or strong current) will cause too many problems and require constant adjustment of the warps. But the method will often provide the most comfortable and quiet berth on a rocky coast.

Anchorage south of Lavezzi, in the Straits of Bonifaccio. Without the line from the stern, the ketch would be unable to lie in such a confined position.

Fore and aft mooring in narrow waters

The method consists of mooring to two anchors, the first cable forward, secured in the bows, the second aft, secured astern. The boat is thus held in place, without swinging at all.

Advantages: this technique permits a boat to moor in a narrow channel, a small creek or a river. Boats made fast in this way run no risk of getting beam on to the current, of touching a hazard or of fouling another boat while swinging, as long as everyone is moored in the same way.

Disadvantages: this method of mooring works well as long as the boat is held exactly parallel to wind and current: it becomes dangerous if wind or current turn and come beam on. If this happens, the strain on the anchors becomes very severe, as the forces work on the boat and cables as on a bowstring (this principle is used when swigging a sheet or halyard without a winch, hauling the line sideways and then recovering the slack around a cleat). A study of the chapter on the forces acting on anchors will also remind the reader that the least windage of a yacht is presented when head to wind. This type of moor is therefore only practicable in light breezes or head to wind, with parallel current, unless the holding is provided by permanent moorings or piles driven into the bottom, as found along the banks of the Hamble. But this relates more to the question of permanent moorings than anchoring; we shall return to this later.

A winch on the afterdeck can be use for tensioning the stern warp. Phote facing page: a convenient palm tree provides far better holding than the heaviest of anchors, above all if it is growing in Cook Bay, Moorea.

Fore and after mooring

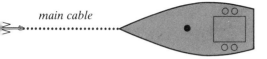
main cable

at lying to a cable secured at the bow

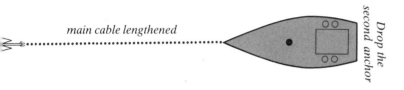
main cable lengthened

Drop the second anchor

ngthen the forward cable: drop second anchor from stern

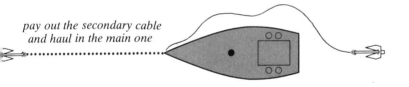
pay out the secondary cable and haul in the main one

turn to original position veering the second cable

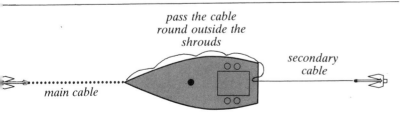
pass the cable round outside the shrouds

secondary cable

main cable

arry the after cable round to the stern, take up slack and secure

Method It can be done in a single manoeuvre, the stern anchor being let go first on a rope cable which is then veered to its maximum length to reach the position to drop the bow anchor. The cables are then adjusted so that the boat lies at an equal distance from each anchor.

One important point: it seems to me preferable to pay out the secondary cable after the main one, allowing the rope to run the length of the hull, on deck but outside the stanchions. It is then secured to a stern cleat (see the sketches opposite). This makes it easier to weigh anchor when getting under way, and allows the boat to be swung through 180° if the wind changes, or a fork moor to be adopted if the gusts become heavy, assuming space allows. Personally I never have much confidence in this method, and I only use it with the stern cable slack to maintain position when space is limited.

Anchoring in the dinghy

Let him to whom this incident has never happened throw the first shackle. Scene: a crowded port. Cast: crew and skipper, just arrived after a passage. Scenario: the boat is to anchor from the bow and then fall back and insert herself between two other yachts already lying bow to anchor, stern to quay. The first act passes without dramas: the tour of inspection is made, the berth examined, then the anchor is got ready while a crew member, on orders from the skipper, takes the dinghy painter forward (until then the dinghy was towing astern) so

that it will not get in the way when reversing. With the painter made fast to the second stanchion on the port side and the boat correctly aligned, the helmsman goes astern. 'Let go' cries the skipper, as the quay begins to approach at a good pace. The reassuring rattle of the chain steadily paying out proves that his order has been carried out to the second. Twenty yards, forty yards, the boat moves into her berth. 'Stop the chain!' Motor in neutral, gipsy immobilised, the boat continues backwards towards the wall of granite. 'Hold that windlass!' 'The brake's full on!' 'Motor ahead!' Crash! ... Too late. The stern has smashed into a projection of the quay under the amused gaze

While anchoring, the painter of the dinghy must be kept as short as possible, to avoid any risk of its catching in the propeller – a classic. Here, an emergency kedge anchor is stowed in the dinghy, ready for instant use in case of need.

of attentive neighbours. 'Haul in the slack forward!' yells the skipper hurling himself towards the bows. 'You veered too much chain!' Well, more than enough had been paid out, certainly. The Zodiac, directly under the bow, is practically foundering under the weight of 240 lb of galvanised chain, coiled like spaghetti with the anchor coyly peeping out from underneath.

Next time, make sure there is

The force and direction of the stream south of Guernsey can be clearly seen on this chart. At three knots at springs, it may seriously disturb our anchorages round the island of Sark.

...er under the bow before letting ...he anchor. . . .

Problems of anchorage in tidal waters

The movement of the sea caused by the tides does not only affect the speed of our boats and add another variable to the dead reckoning equations: it also poses problems when, after one or more days at sea, we want to take a few hours of well-deserved rest.

● **Choice of anchorage** When deciding where to anchor, it is important to find out from the tables and charts what is the range of tide and speed of currents in the light of the day's tidal range, especially if the tides are near springs. Certain deeply indented bays and estuaries may offer excellent protection against sea and swell, but often suffer from very rapid streams at full flood or ebb, frequently accompanied by turbulences which can break up their general direction into counter-currents, eddies and whirlpools. Information on these is not always easy to come by, but there are large-scale tidal charts for many of the more important harbours, and other notes often appear in pilot books and other nautical works.

The greater the range of the tide, the longer the scope must be to allow for the changes in depth (see sketch on page 142). However, this length of scope can then produce a very large swinging circle at low water, a factor that must be taken into account when choosing the anchoring position.

● **Method of anchoring** The technique of the approach and the operations that must be carried out before letting go described above can be seriously hampered by a strong current. Whether it is ahead, across or against, its presence will always complicate the process of anchoring, particularly if this is being carried out under sail. Keep a close eye on boats already at anchor, buoys, fishing floats, or the little eddies that appear downstream of obstacles such as rocks, beacons or piles. They usually provide excellent clues to the direction and speed of the current.

If the directions of wind and tide are the same, then always approach facing into them for as long as the surroundings permit. If they are different, the direction produced by the combination of the two determines the tactics to be adopted. This can be gauged by the way other boats are lying if the anchorage is already in use. Approach on a course parallel to the way they are lying, then fall back, paying out the cable. Only experience and common sense will provide a guide to the exact method to adopt in each individual situation, a statement that can be extended to apply to many manoeuvres made in strongly tidal waters.

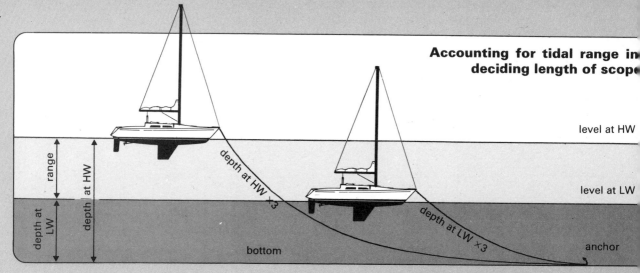

Accounting for tidal range in deciding length of scope

level at HW

level at LW

range

depth at HW

depth at LW

depth at HW ×3

depth at LW ×3

anchor

bottom

Above: to be sure of a long enough scope for a boat anchored in waters with a large tidal range, the length of the cable veered must be based on the depth at high water.

Right: too short a scope can cause the anchor to drag at high tide.

Below: possible effects of the reversal of the tidal stream on the orientation of an anchored boat, which can vary with the strength of the wind. The sketches are schematic: the irregularity of the combinations of the two elements will usually create less formal results.

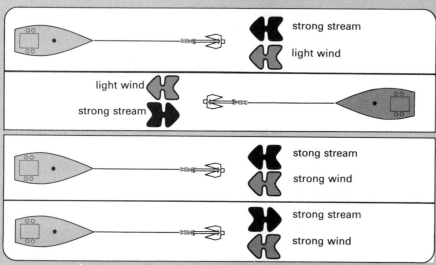

strong stream

light wind

light wind

strong stream

stong stream

strong wind

strong stream

strong wind

● **Scope** As we can now see, changing the depth of water, considerable tidal range will inevitably affect the ratio between depth and scope. Thus, if one were to anchor using three times the depth when the sounder was reading fifteen feet at low water in Jersey, i.e. veering forty-five feet of cable, one would suffer a nasty shock when the water level had risen by ten metres at the end of a spring flood; by then the anchor would be a-trip, and the boat free to drift at will. It is always safer to veer too much cable rather than too little, and a careful eye should be kept on the holding of the anchor and the reactions of the boat during the different phases of the tide (1).

If swinging room is restricted, it may be necessary to adjust the cable at regular intervals in line with the changes in depth, even if this means that a night watch has to be set. Or go and dry out at the top of the bay (see page 159), with all the constraints imposed by such an option.

To my mind, it is still better to stay afloat.

(1) See the first book in this collection Sailing, the Course, the Route and the Position by Alain Grée.

142

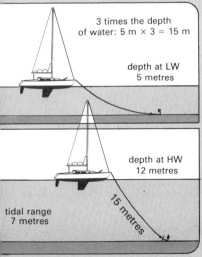

3 times the depth
of water: 5 m × 3 = 15 m

depth at LW
5 metres

depth at HW
12 metres

tidal range
7 metres

15 metres

● **Holding of the anchor** As well as the variations in depth due to the tidal range, which constantly modify the ratio of the scope to the depth of water, there is another important factor which upsets the holding of an anchor in tidal waters: the changing direction of the traction effort. If the wind is not strong enough to override the effects of the stream, the turn of the tide can produce a 180° change in the direction of pull on the cable. This change of direction sometimes causes flat-bladed anchors to break out by turning over when the forces are strong. Additionally, the risk of fouling the anchor, rare with modern designs but possible on very firm bottoms, can arise, with the danger of dragging. One should also note the danger of chafe against rough places on the bottom if a mixed cable is in use, due to the change of direction at each turn of the tide, and the possibility of the cable (rope or chain) ultimately getting caught under some rock or other snag on the bottom, with all the problems that then occur as the tide rises.

All in all, the number of variables added to the general anchoring problem by the presence of a major tidal rise and fall require considerable added vigilance from skipper and crew. And those who practice these arts regularly usually acquire a high degree of seamanship.

143

Always give preference to fenders of lenticular shape when mooring alongside a quay or another boat. There are two reasons for this: they do not roll (with the risk of ejection), and they do not act as a combined ink-pad and rubber stamp, transferring colour or dirt from one hull to the other. And some neighbours are coated with filth that is positively indelible. . . . Right: two boats lying to a single anchor in Funchal Bay, on the delightful island of Madeira.

masts must overlap, not coincide

open angle as in a fork moor

breast-ropes
slightly slack,
springs taut

Rafting up in a pair on two anchors; leave some slack on the breast-ropes and tighten the springs with winches to limit movement as far as possible. Keep an eye on the position of the masts to avoid collision between the sets of rigging, because while the crews are having a drink, you don't want it to be the spreaders that do the clinking. . . .

With land breeze

WIND

anchor

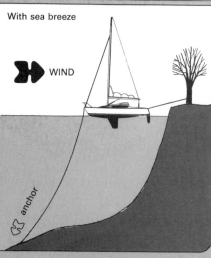

With sea breeze

WIND

anchor

Rafting up at anchor

One should only use this techn in good weather, and when the absolutely no swell. When breeze blows gently on a shelt area of water protected waves, one may then raft up one anchor down per boat, cables at a slightly open ang form a sort of false fork moor the springs take the principal st and be careful to position the b in such a way that if they accidentally roll, the shrouds not collide.

Inshore short-cable anchorage

Although rare in tidal waters, kind of anchorage is quite o met with in the Mediterranean for example, in the famous D Pitons Bay anchorage in the V Indies. In these anchorages, shore is so steep-to that the and can only find bottom a few me out from the beach. After mak sure that there is no underw obstruction lurking near the sh it is necessary to anchor as cl inshore as possible, then run a ashore to limit the swinging ran (Preferably attach this to someth solid.)

Stories

1

Perlette in the Aegean

This moving account shows once again how dangerous it is to leave a boat at anchor in strong wind. It is taken from the charming book by Marthe Oulié and Hermine de Saussure, which describes the cruise made by these two young yachtswomen across the Aegean in 1925 aboard the *Perlette*, with nobody but themselves aboard (from *The Cruise of the Perlette*, Hachette, 1926).

'*Returning to* Perlette, *we were almost blinded by the hot wind which blew violently from the land, breaking a branch from a fig-tree as we watched. . . .*

'*On the jetty, we found all the men gathered together, shouting and waving their arms in the air, and communicating their fear to their wives who broke down in sobs. Terrible gusts screamed in the rigging of the caïques which, little by little dragging their anchors, were being driven dangerously close to each other. The wind was so strong that one could hardly stand on the jetty without holding on to something.*

'*The moon illuminated that strange and beautiful spectacle of a storm in a port. Less than a hundred yards from shore, the squalls were creating an* enormous sea, from which masses of spray rose like clouds, leaping up to the height of Perlette's masthead, which showed up against the sky above the far shore. We strained our eyes to see whether Perlette too was dragging her anchor.

'*After five minutes we were convinced of it. Now, the rocks were only fifty yards from where she was anchored: within an hour she would strike. At all costs we had to get back aboard, put down another anchor and get a warp ashore. But the frightened sailors hesitated to take us out to her in their heavy boats, so strongly did the women of the port plead with them to stay ashore. And still* Perlette *moved* slowly to her doom. At last, swaye our entreaties and taking advanta a slight lull, the men gave way to insistence and took us aboard in best boat, after fitting themselves with spare oars for a fifty yard pass

'*After a good hour of manoeu backwards and forwards across hellish sea, we succeeded in la down a huge borrowed an attached by all the warps w aboard. The men left, and we were at last to stretch out on our bunks sleep, in spite of the infernal mus the wind in the shrouds, and bucking of* Perlette *as she rode to anchors.*'

Isle of Lipso, 5th–10th July 1

2

Anahita in Tierra del Fuego

...uary 1937. Commander Louis ...nicot, alone aboard his cutter ...ahita, entered the Maggellan ...ait. Met by squalls and willi-...ws ever since his arrival off the ...ospitable shores of Tierra del ...go, he had to fight a long battle ...inst a violent current that drove ...back at every tack. Exhausted, ...decided at last to anchor at the ...d of a sandy creek, taking a line ...ore.

...nce the operation was completed, ...dn't linger on deck. I changed into ...clothes, and then fell into a deep ... ... after two nights without ...p, and what nights!

...was awakened by a series of ...nps on the hull; once awake I ...ised that I was being hailed from ...shore. Hurrying on deck, I saw ...ral pebbles that had been thrown ...n the shore. Looking around me, I ...struck by the change that had taken ...e in the appearance of the sur-...ndings; the tide had fallen greatly, ...the steeply sloping beach seemed ...aordinarily high. A cable or so to

seaward the surface of the sea was carpeted with bladderwrack; beneath the boat I could see the bottom clearly: I was about to touch, and that was what they were shouting at me from the beach. I didn't mind the cutter drying, but not without her legs, for at Caran-tac I had been assured that if I allowed her to lie over when she dried out, she would not lift again on the flood!

'Hastily I rigged the legs: too late! The keel was already hard aground and, to add to my ill luck, Anahita had already begun to heel the wrong way, that is to say, down the slope. On the beach, three men watched my every movement. No doubt to prove their desire to help, they offered to take another line ashore. This time one of them waded into the water up to the armpits to catch the end: brave chap! The apprehension I had first felt about the situation did not last: it is imposs-ible, I said to myself, that she will not come up with the tide. Even so, I took care to close all hatches well before the water rose to the rail when, gradually, Anahita righted herself.'

(From The Cruise of Anahita by Louis Bernicot, Gallimard 1939.)

Above: a photo of the cutter Anahita, which I came across two years ago in a West Indian anchorage, with a remodelled doghouse but in perfect condition.
Centre, right: Louis Bernicot after his single-handed circumnavigation.

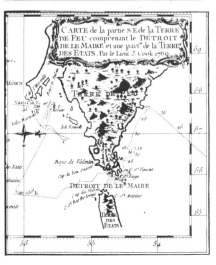

Weighing anchor

Except in cases where an emergency departure has to be made for some reason, getting under way generally presents fewer difficulties than the operations that have to be carried out before anchoring. Even so, it is a manoeuvre that needs to be thought out, and requires to be done in a series of phases as precise as those for anchoring.

Preparation for departure

One generally weighs anchor to leave a shelter, and thus to regain the open sea. So it is no use hoping to tidy up on deck or below once *out* of the anchorage; that is where the protection from wind and sea is, which is why you chose it in the first place. And to infer from what you can observe at anchor what the conditions will be like outside would involve a command of occult sciences. Everyone learns in the end that it can easily be blowing a gentle force 2 in the shelter of a comfortable creek, and a very brisk 7 in the open sea – (this begins to stick in the mind after the second or third time you have had to replace the genoa with the number two jib after the first half mile).

So before considering weighing anchor, it is important to call to mind the different actions that have

Who has not felt that oncoming panic when, as bad weather approaches, the anchor refuses to break out close to a rocky lee shore. . . .

to be carried out before all departures:

- clear up on deck and below
- listen to the forecast (if possible)
- everyone into seagoing kit
- hank on the appropriate sails, trying to remember that it is always less trouble to get out a bigger sail than to shorten what you have set already
- leave the tender afloat, ready to haul aboard once the anchor is aweigh (it will be useful in case of difficulty in weighing)
- check up on the route for leaving, and if need be the course to be steered once clear of the land
- check fuel, oil, battery and heat exchanger (if fitted) levels
- make a note of the lights that will be relevant if the passage is likely to extend after dark
- check that halyards and sheets are attached, free and ready
- close hatches and portholes.

All that is routine, you may remark. And you are right. But it is as well to recall sometimes that a boat should always be ready to face bad weather, even if the barometer is high and steady. And you only have to watch some boats getting under way to realise that not everyone always applies these elementary rules.

To break out and then recover an anchor almost always presents difficulties when the bottom is foul with rocks or other anchor chains – difficulties which get worse as the wind increases.

1

Weighing one anchor under power

To get a better understanding of the operations directly connected with weighing anchor, let us first consider the manoeuvre under power. This will simplify the subsequent study of weighing anchor under sail.

(1) Take the strain off the cable by motoring ahead, at low speed, towards a point vertically above the presumed position of the anchor. At this stage it is important to give the helmsman clear instructions by means of agreed signs for ahead, port, starboard, stop etc., avoiding verbal orders which will be lost in the noise of the wind, especially if they are delivered with the back turned.

(2) Haul in the cable, either by hand or using the windlass. Bear in mind that if there is a wind, the windage will create a serious resistance to your efforts; as soon as the cable tightens, take a turn round the samson post or cleat and signal the helmsman to move on towards the anchor.

(3) When the anchor is a-trip (scope reduced to the depth of the water), haul more strongly to break out the anchor, i.e. disengage it from the bottom. From this moment the helmsman should be running the engine ahead, to stop the boat from falling back with the gusts, or drifting with the current. He should aim to stand still or move forward very slowly.

(4) Haul the anchor aboard, cleaning it if necessary if it has mud on its flukes (an excellent way of doing this is to leave it suspended just below the surface while the boat covers one or two hundred yards at low speed).

(5) Stow the cable, sealing the chain pipe if bad weather is expected, and locking the gipsy where appropriate.

(6) Secure the anchor to its support, even if it is held on the stemhead by its chain. This can always jump off the gipsy or come loose from the cleat to which it has been made fast. Having encountered several misadventures of this sort in head seas, I always recommend an independant lashing for this purpose (see page 74), because, if the ratchet of the windlass jumps free under the shock of a wave, you could have fifty fathoms of chain over the side, with the CQR at the end pretending to be a sea anchor, if the attachment of the bitter end does not give way first.

The four phases of weighing anchor

anchor

shortening the ca

anchor a-t

anchor broken

Weighing two anchors from a fork moor

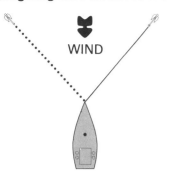

The boat is lying to two anchors   *Recover the chain cable, paying out the other*   *Then recover the second cable*

2

Weighing under power from a two-anchor moor

a fork moor, one must first
in the all-chain cable, paying
he other line as necessary so
allow the boat to bring the
anchor a-trip. Once that has
got aboard, the second
or is weighed in the ordinary
er.

anchor is backed, everything
nds on how this was done. If
ength of the joining chain is
er than the depth of water, the
ors are hauled up one by one.
wise one must take a deep
h and haul them both up
her, unless the precaution was
to put a tripping line on the

hanked to the forestay can often
iously hamper work in the bows.
the halyard to lift the hanks and
clear the foredeck.

backing anchor. In that case one
can haul in alternately a length of
line and then a length of chain,
supporting the weight of each
anchor in turn while raising the
other (see page 128).

It is also possible to raise the
kedge anchor from the tender if
there are doubts about manoeuvring under power. Here as elsewhere, I believe that every situation
calls for its own solution according
to wind and current, weather, the
position of the boat relative to any
dangers, the quality of lifting tackle
available, and the experience and
number of the crew.

Reminder: three rules must be
observed, whatever the method
used:

(1) reduce the strain on the cable
as it is recovered by motoring
gently ahead,

(2) do not go beyond the point
where the cable is up and down,
to avoid damaging the bows by
scraping them with the chain,

(3) be ready to snatch a turn on
the cable if it tightens, for example if the boat falls back under
the influence of a gust.

The five phases of weighing anchor under sail

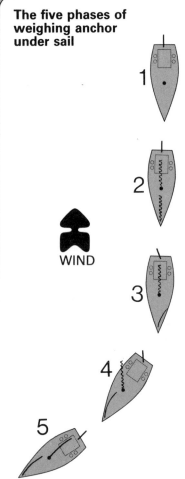

WIND

(1) *Boat at anchor: the crew tidies up and prepares the chosen sails for hoisting.*
(2) *Jib and mainsail are hoisted and allowed to flap. Begin to haul in the cable.*
(3) *The boat is moving up towards the anchor: back the jib lightly and continue to haul in.*
(4) *Anchor a-trip: with the jib aback and the tiller up, tack the jib to the correct side. The anchor breaks out: haul it up as quickly as possible.*
(5) *Anchor abroad, haul in the mainsheet, we're off! Stow anchor and cable before reaching the open sea.*

3

Weighing anchor under sail

This can be done in all weath
small boats, but on bigger
only in light airs, because w
motor the crew will only hav
strength of his own muscles
alone or through a manual
lass to recover the anchor
during the operation there v
the extra windage from the
hoisted and flapping, which i
siderable.

A Principle of the manoeuvre

The boat lying head to wind o
anchor (if there are two in us
secondary one should firs
raised with the help of the te
the jib and mainsail are hoiste
allowed to flap with freed s
Then the cable is hauled
whatever means are available
the anchor is brought aboard
which the sails are sheeted i
the boat got under way.

*the sketches given here can
...al with generalised situations; it
...ossible to illustrate the exact
...ue to adopt in each individual
...t may occur. Their real purpose
...aid to thinking in advance
...e general problems of weighing
...il. The exact method chosen
...end to a large extent on the
...ual characteristics of each boat:
...e pay off easily or carry weather
...oes she drift straight back or
...ickly away from the wind? Only
...nce will tell.*

Preparation for the manoeuvre

...al to what has already been
...bed, except that the hoisting
...ontrol of the sails has to be
... Begin with the mainsail,
... or not, according to the
... If there is enough searoom
..., this one sail will be enough,
...ularly if the way out from the
...rage lies on a reach or a run.
...wise one must add the jib,
...y to assure immediate
...euvrability when the anchor
... out, and partly to enable the
...) get off on the correct tack by
...g the jib if necessary: this
... vital. The sketches opposite
...one method of proceeding.

Weighing anchor

...flapping, sheets free, the
...g in of the cable is begun,
...a crew member stands ready
...d the jib aback on the side
...ite to the desired tack when
...der is given. In strong winds
...hase of the operation is long
...ring as the windage of the
...nd sails produces a major
...nt of resistance. A turn round
...h may be necessary.

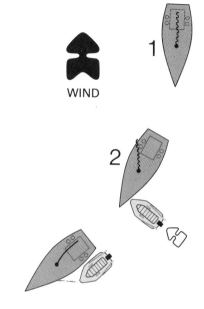

Weighing anchor under mainsail alone with the aid of the tender

WIND

1

2

*(1) Hauling in the cable, mainsail set and flapping.
(2) Anchor a-trip, the motor tender pushes the boat's head round onto the correct tack.
(3) Broken out! haul in anchor, recover tender, sheet in the main and hoist jib.*

When the anchor breaks out, there are two possibilities.

• The boat pays off on the correct tack (the crewman in charge of the jib having provided gentle aid by just holding the jib aback by just the necessary amount): the rest of the cable must be recovered as quickly as possible, so that the anchor does not snag on an obstacle if it was not quite vertically below the stem when it broke out, and the sails sheeted in to get straight under way.

• The boat pays off on the wrong tack: the cable must be veered and the boat re-anchored without delay. Then start again.

An ingenious solution, if you have the luck to be equipped with an outboard-powered inflatable: help the boat to pay off on the right tack by pressure on the bow at the crucial moment from the nose of the dinghy. The force produced in such a way is surprising, even with the smallest outboard.

Weighing under sail with dangers close downwind

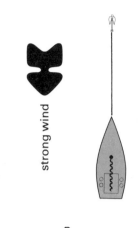

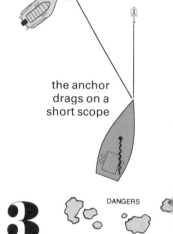

strong wind

let go!

the anchor drags on a short scope

DANGERS

DANGERS

DANGERS

1

While weighing, the reduction of the scope combined with the effect of windage can cause the anchor to drag without properly breaking out. Without the aid of an auxiliary, there can be a risk of being carried down onto the rocks before gaining steerage way.

2

To overcome this danger, have the dinghy standing by to windward of the boat, equipped with an anchor shackled to a buoyant line. If the wind is strong, it may be advisable to hold the dinghy on a Grapnel. Only after taking this precaution should one begin to shorten the main cable.

3

The main cable is hauled in. If no problems arise, the dinghy is hauled on its floating cable and recovered while the boat is sailing out of the anchorage. If, however, the anchor drags, the crewman in the dinghy go the kedge, on which the boat c held until the main anchor is recovered.

Note: certain situations present particular problems in getting under way, notably when, as a result of dragging or swinging, the boat finds herself with dangers close under her lee. If no motor is available, it is then wise to take precautions before risking shortening the cable and possibly encouraging the anchor to drag while still holding sufficiently to prevent the boat from steering. In this event a kedge can be carried out and laid a safe distance to windward, enabling the main anchor to be recovered and the boat then to be got under way from the second anchor. Or as a minimum precaution, the kedge can be held in readiness to let go from the dinghy if the main anchor does drag. Buoyant cable is useful for this task, and the man should be ready to l instantly if the boat begins to onto the rocks.

In practice, outside s schools it is rare nowadays beginner to attempt anchor oeuvres under sail; common demands that he should first under power before profiting the experience gained to e ment with sail alone, at first in weather and then, after years, in all conditions.

But these manoeuvres shou practised under sail as ofte possible; not only for the lo the art, but also to gain exper against the day when a me ical failure may make it necessary.

Chain problems

Tricky departure from the old port of St Tropez: while weighing anchor, the skipper of the motor cruiser discovers that it is foul under the chain of the yacht moored stern to quay. Thanks to a powerful winch, the whole lot is lifted to the surface. It is then only ncessary to pass a bight of rope under the offending chain to free the anchor. Casting off one end of the bight then returns the yacht chain to the bottom.

155

BEAUFORT WIND SCALE				
Beaufort Number	Mean Wind Speed equivalent in knots	Descriptive Terms	Height of waves (in m)	
			Probable	Maximum
0	Less than 1	Calm	–	–
1	1–3	Light air	–	–
2	4–6	Light breeze	0.15	0.30
3	7–10	Gentle breeze	0.60	1.00
4	11–16	Moderate breeze	1.00	1.50
5	17–21	Fresh breeze	1.80	2.50
6	22–27	Strong breeze	3.00	4.00
7	28–33	Near gale	4.00	6.00
8	34–40	Gale	5.50	7.50
9	41–47	Strong gale	7.00	9.75
10	48–55	Storm	9.00	12.50
11	56–63	Violent storm	11.30	16.00
12	64 +	Hurricane	13.70	–

Weighing anchor before getting under way is never easy when it is blowing hard, because one must struggle against the boat's windage to reach the point where the anchor will break out. To do this without power in 30 knots of breeze requires solid muscles. Things get even worse if the cable is trapped under another boat's chain. One solution is to use the tender's grapnel.

Freeing a cable trapped under a chain with the help of a grapnel

1 *A common problem when getting under way: the cable is trapped under the chain of a boat which has come and anchored since your arrival. And, naturally, his chain is much heavier than yours!*

2 *If the windlass is not strong enough, one can add an extra purchase by attaching a rope to the chain and using a winch to help the windlass. Or make use of a grapnel to hook up the offending chain.*

3 This chain, once caught, will be partially hauled up from the stem or the dinghy, according to circumstances, so as to disengage the imprisoned cable. It is often advisable to replace the grapnel with a bight when the chain can be reached.

4 If it is necessary to adjust the position of the support, a rope bight will slide along the chain more easily than the grapnel. It is rare for the operation to succeed at the first attempt. It is inadvisable to anchor inside harbours because this problem arises so frequently.

Burning off and scrubbing a fishing boat hull towards the beginning of the century, at a period when neither travel lifts nor electric sanders existed. Below, a Kelt 707 balanced on its retractable mini-keels.

Drying out

Let us choose our words with care: just as you can run a mile or run a tap, so you can dry out an alcoholic or against a quay. The verb stays the same, only the action is different! But whatever happens, let us not confuse drying out with going aground: we dry out our boats of our own free will, whereas one goes aground on a shoal accidentally. The distinction is important, and if the skipper says he decided to dry out, you had better not talk about him having gone aground!

Why dry out?

One dries out a boat for three main reasons:

● to take shelter in a basin that dries at low water because there is no deep water anchorage in the neighbourhood

● to scrub the hull between two tides, in waters where there is sufficient tidal range

● to avoid foundering when, after sustaining damage, the crew is unable to fother a leak well enough to prevent the inflow of water gaining on the pumps.
   In each of these cases, the decision is taken voluntarily by the skipper, with a view to safety or convenience, so we are dealing with drying out or beaching, not grounding.

How do we dry out?

Drying on legs

Although monohulls generally have longitudinal stability when standing on their keel, they usually need some form of lateral support. Apart from twin-keel boats or the few with flat bottoms and lifting keels, they need the aid of specially designed legs. These consist of two pieces of wood or metal hinged to the main beam and supported by fore and aft guys so that they are held vertical, with their bases (to which broad feet are attached) at the level of the bottom of the keel. Different fixing systems are used according to the types of boat (which are becoming less and less numerous) that are so equipped, but all are based on this principle of double lateral support.

Drying out alongside a quay

No need for legs (or maybe just a single one as a safeguard); it is the vertical wall against which it leans that supports the boat. The technique is simple: protect the freeboard with cylindrical fenders, making sure they do not get out of position as the tide falls, and run an adjustable line from the mast to the quay to preserve the vertical equilibrium. As long as a careful eye is kept on everything during the ebb and the flood, there is no reason for anything to go wrong, as the bollards on the quay can be used at any time to support the bow or stern if a problem of longitudinal stability should suddenly arise. It is important to check up on the underwater parts of the quay or jetty, as these sometimes sport dangerous protrusions. The ideal is to make a reconnaissance at the low water of the preceding tide.

Precautions

Three essential points to watch before allowing the boat to dry out on a falling tide:

● the uniformity of the soil on which the legs will rest, which must be sufficiently firm to prevent one leg from sinking in unevenly (there is nothing quite like that for providing an upsetting spectacle. . . .),

● the horizontality of the bottom, both longitudinally and laterally, to avoid the boat heeling too much, or leaning too far forward or back. Too much inclination, apart from the risk of loss of balance, can actually allow the boat to fill as the tide rises,

● the absence of obstructions under the keel or legs, which could produce loss of balance as the boat dries.

There is only one way to get the chances on one's side a[nd] avoid these sombre possibilitie[s]: observe the composition and la[y] out of the bottom by soundi[ng] meticulously with a lead or a po[le] or by diving with a mask if t[he] water is clear and warm enoug[h]. And make sure you explore t[he] exact part of the bottom that y[ou] are going to dry on.

Where do we dry out?

Somewhere where the tidal ran[ge] is at least equal to the draft of t[he] boat, so that the bottom is entire[ly] uncovered at low water. Choose [a] site well protected from swell a[nd] chop, firstly to enable the positio[n]ing of the boat to be done [as] accurately as possible, and secon[d]ly to avoid the risk of poundi[ng] while drying or floating off. On[ce] the basin has been chosen, the ne[xt] thing is to find a patch of botto[m] that is smooth and flat. The be[st] bottoms to dry on are general[ly] sand, gravel or shingle; mud [is] inadvisable because it can b[e] treacherous, allowing a leg to si[nk] in or concealing a rock or a piece [of] wreckage below its surface. Natu[r]ally, if you can find a coveri[ng] causeway that dries at low wate[r,] display your disc and park witho[ut] hesitation!

…out legs, lying against a quay re-
…es the risks inherent in the drying
…procedure. Always pay attention to
…and aft support in the case of
…t-keeled yachts, especially if the
…or is fitted right aft.

When do we
dry out?

…u will find the answer in the Tide
…les, which tell you the times and
…ges of the day's tides. Anyone
…o has ever watched a bath
…ptying will understand that one
…st take advantage of the ebb to
…the work. Thank you, Mr
…himedes. A calculation of tidal
…ghts can even establish the ex-
…moment at which the keel will
…ch bottom, and when the boat
…be afloat again: I would even
…gest that by subtracting the first
…re from the second, you will be
…e to estimate the time available
…your repainting. . . .

…rning: if you dry out where there
…ttle depth for you at high water,
…ke sure that the tides are mak-
…i.e. that the following range
…be bigger. If they are taking off,
…will risk being neaped and
…ing to wait until they make
…in before you can resume your
…rrupted cruise. That is, unless
…dried on an equinoctial
…ng. . . .

…fact, drying out a boat always
…olves some risk. Jean Bluche
…reason to thank the god Nep-
…e the day he set his keel on the
…ch of the island of Tarawa in the
…t Pacific. Without the support of
…y or legs, he must have had
…t confidence both in the
…ness of the bottom and in pro-
…nce to dare this manoeuvre.

'We arrived on 11th December, the
day of the spring tide, and we wanted
to scrub. So the next day I steered
Chimère into the port in order to look
for a suitable place. . . . An hour later
the choice was made and the boat
grounded, then dried. We set up guys
to the masthead on both sides and
waited for the water level to fall. At
about 1500 the owner of the boatyard
asked me if I wasn't going to fit legs,
and I answered that usually I just held
her up by guys from the mast, and that
Chimère had a fairly wide straight
keel. If he had said then that the bottom
was not very firm and that there was a
slight declivity where we were, our
misfortunes would have been avoided.

'We had practically finished the port
side when Suzanne shouted "She's
moving!". Jean-Guillaume and I, who
were still scraping the bottom and keel,
jumped backwards more from curios-
ity than fear, but we had hardly
straightened up when we saw the boat
gather speed and crash down at our

feet: the starboard masthead guy had
given way. A moment after the first
shock of the hull hitting the earth came
a second, sharper crack: the mast
collapsed onto a passenger launch beside us. . . . By the light of the lamp I
dismantled the mast, unscrewing the
rigging screws. It would have been
more sensible to empty the boat, if only
to lighten her, but I still felt confident
because no crack was visible. But alas,
when the tide rose, the evidence had to
be admitted: some planks were sprung
and the water was pouring in at a fair
rate along some of the seams.'

By sheer luck, because the
weather remained fine and Chimère was a well-built boat, he
succeeded in getting her upright as
the tide rose, and in finishing his
circumnavigation with all his
planks in place (from The Voyage of
the Chimère by Jean Bluche,
Reschly 1962).

161

Permanent moorings

long stay at anchor away from
...t, as for example when winter-
...n a sheltered creek or estuary,
...rmanent mooring is to be re-
...nended. This method of secur-
...gives greater safety to a boat
...is to be left to herself for a
...thy period. However, the time
...money involved in its creation
...laying must be available, and
...is generally the major obstacle
...he adoption of what is un-
...btedly one of the most reliable
...s of mooring.
...cal regulations must, of
...se, be studied and any neces-
...permissions obtained before a
...nanent mooring can be laid. It
...ld be impossible in a book
...gned for the international mar-
...o give details here, but in any
...try it will be obligatory to leave
...main channels clear, and in
...e crowded areas (the south and
...coasts of England, for exam-
...it would be virtually impossi-
...for a private individual to get
...nission to lay a mooring, as all
...lable space has been used up.
...ne most commonly used
...hods of securing a permanent
...ring are:

...oncrete blocks

...ushroom anchors

...orkscrew piles.

A fourth solution consists of getting hold of one or more old ship's
anchors from a chandler at a big
port. This happended to me in
1977, when for 300 francs my friend
Jack Grout found me, from a local
scrap-iron merchant, a huge 176 lb
Grapnel, which held *Pitcairn* firmly
anchored in the Old Basin for a
whole winter. Anchored along with
a fishing boat, it valiantly resisted
not only bad weather, but also the
effects of the harbour authorities'
dredger. It is still there, to the great
delight of the unknown skipper
who has inherited it.

Unless you can make a similar
lucky find, you will probably have
to resort to the commonest solution: a sunken concrete block. So
let us examine its characteristics.

Concrete block moorings

There are no regulations for the
specifications of permanent moorings, either as regards their shape
or their weight. But of course these
should be suitable for the size of
the boat which they are going to
have to hold, and will vary with
their number and the nature of the
bottom; two or three blocks buried
well under the surface will be more
resistant than a single one simply
sitting on the bottom. And so each
can be considerably lighter.

To determine the average weight
needed for a block, it seems sensible to return to the breaking strains
of anchor chains (see the table on
page 33).

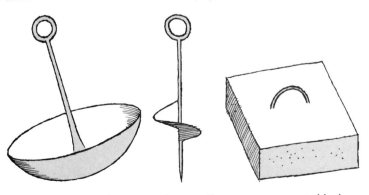

mushroom anchor   *corkscrew pile*   *concrete block*

Right, a solution to the problem *picking up a mooring buoy, usually* *rich in acrobatic gymnastics. Thank* *a retaining clip, a mobile hook on* *end of a warp is attached to* *mooring ring before being relea* *from the boathook. This is all d* *automatically, and at a distan*

Equipment

● **Ring:** in order to be able to t the mooring chain, the block m be provided with an attachm point to which it can be shackle reinforcing bar sunk into the bl is the ideal solution, as long as gauge and method of fixing adequate to the strains that will imposed. There is no disadvanta if it is a bit too big, so go for a hea fitting here, and avoid any worr afterwards.

● **Chain:** no need to bother wit chain of great length, because if bottom-weight is up to its job it a resistance that removes the cessity for a normal scope. Depe ing on the swinging room, one a a half times to twice the depth reasonable, taking the greatest c if the tidal range is considerable the waters in question. In that ca the calculations must be based the highest tide of the year (equinoctial spring). The ch should be of the same weight the regulation main anchor cha as the length of the scope has effect on the strength of each i vidual link. However, if the wate subject to regular changes stream direction as a result of t the risk of abrasion against bottom requires that the chain s be one grade thicker than wo otherwise be needed: i.e. $5/16''$ mm) in place of $1/4''$ (6.3 mm), e

An interesting detail is that as never in contact with the air

---

Extent of swinging circle

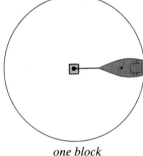

one block

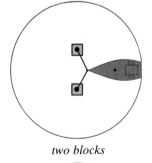

two blocks

three blocks

If a 33 ft yacht requires a chain of $5/16''$ (8 mm) diameter, with a working load of two tonnes (see tables on pages 33 and 34), logic demands that the inert block sitting on the bottom should attain this weight. QED.

Or else it should offer an equal resistance. Thus, a square flat slab will provide twice the holding of a cube of the same weight. Bury it under three feet of mud, and its holding power will be doubled again!

This is what makes it difficult to give exact figures on this subject, even though some authors seem to feel it necessary to defend various arbitrary norms. In my view, accurate calculations would involve parameters so diverse that only a professional in the field of soil mechanics would be able to make them, taking account of the characteristics of the boat, the situation of the haven and the local meteorological and oceanographic conditions. The stakes seem to me too high to do other than err on the safe side, especially when one is dealing with boats over thirty feet in length.

The swinging circle can vary as a *function of the number of underwater* *mooring points. The more numerous* *they are, the less its area need be,* *which can be highly advantageous in* *crowded waters.*

...anently immersed chain cor-
...s only very little, and lasts a
... deal longer than one which
...etimes dries out.
...oy: used only to allow the
...n to be recovered when the
...returns to the mooring. Diffe-
...methods can be used to join it
...ne chain: shackled to a link,
...l to an independent tripping
...or directly attached to the end
...ne chain. In the last case a
...al type of buoy must be used
... a metal rod passing right
...ugh it, joining the end of the
...n to the mooring warp from the
...
...refer to avoid intermediaries,
...ring the boat directly on the
...n itself, and leaving the buoy
...l on the deck or secured to the
...stay. This removes one possi-
... point of weakness between
... and bottom-weight.
...wivel: if the boat is simply held
...the bow, a galvanised steel
...ring swivel should be inter-
...ed between the bottom-
...ht's ring and the chain, to
...w the boat to swing through
... without risk of twisting the
...n. Repeated throughout winter,
... movement would produce a
...ere shortening of the chain in
...long run, producing dangerous
...hanical stresses. Make sure
...accessory is of suitable size: its
...king load should at least corres-
...d with that of the chain being
...d.

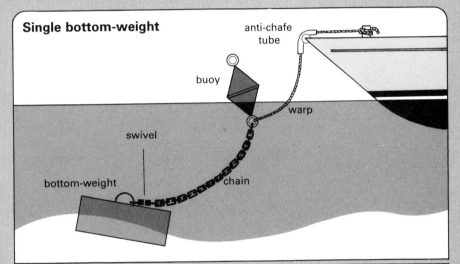

Single bottom-weight

anti-chafe tube

buoy

warp

swivel

bottom-weight

chain

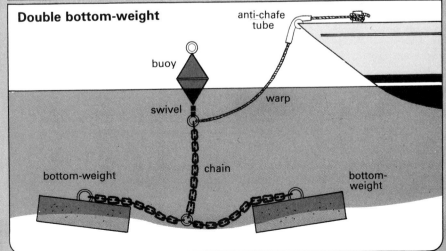

Double bottom-weight

anti-chafe tube

buoy

swivel

warp

bottom-weight

chain

bottom-weight

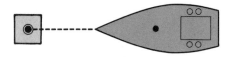

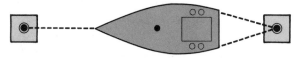

On single bottom-weight. Swinging through 360°, so swivel required.

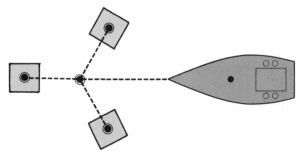

Layout of moorings with one or more bottom-weights

Between two bottom-weights. No swinging, so no swivel.

Three bottom-weights in triple fork. Swingin through 360°.

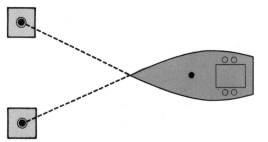

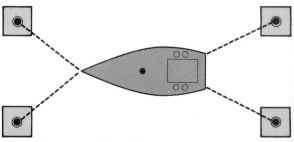

On two forked bottom-weights. Swinging through 360°. Swivel.

Two bottom-weights forward and two astern. N swinging.

Layout of moorings

In order to reduce the swinging circle, one may be led to use several bottom-weights in the construction of one mooring. The sketches above show a number of the different possibilities available. Principally, they consist of:

- a single bottom-weight
- two bottom-weights in the fork. moor position, with a single chain to the boat's bows
- two bottom-weights between which the boat is moored by bow and stern lines
- three bottom-weights in star formation, with a short chain from their centre to the bows (reduced swinging circle, better division of stress, tripled holding power in the event of really bad weather).

The number of bottom-weights used will depend on the method of holding required (with or without swinging) and on the size of each of them. Photo right: a steep anchorage on the Aegean island of Santorin. As the bottom plunges vertically for 300 metres, only a permanent mooring permits boats to lie stern to quay in front of the delightful village of Thira.

Sinking the mooring

The manufacture of submerged blocks differs according to the kind of cement used: old-fashioned slow drying, or protected from marine corrosion by quick drying. Some special types can even dry under water, an advantage which allows the bottom-weight to be poured directly on the bottom at a

low water spring tide, in the case moorings in drying areas.

The traditional method wintering in deep water invol building a box-mould on the she to receive the concrete mixed the purpose. When, after three four days, it is dry, it has to transported to the site. The b solution is to build a raft made empty barrels lashed together, w an improvised plank deck, the id being to pour the concrete as ne ly as possible directly onto t makeshift raft, to reduce amount of manhandling need One may also be able to get help of a fishing boat with a hea winch. Fix the chain to the ring, a let go the whole outfit at the chos site: not forgetting the flotati buoy!

Quite a performance, usua Unforgettable.

At anchor, there is no protection from the furies of wind and sea. Indeed, the worst danger is to believe, after a sojourn of a few weeks passed without problems in an open anchorage, that these apocalyptic squalls only occur occasionally. If during the course of this book I have deliberately cited numerous accounts of disasters that have overtaken ships at anchor, it is not for any love of the sensational, but simply to remind those who so far have never had to face up to its fury that the sea still knows how to destroy our vessels even when they try to escape from its rage by sheltering in a fold of the coast. This last account was written by Commander Gatier at the beginning of the year 1841, when he was in a mission aboard the corvette *La Marne* along the Algerian coast. Dramatic, but full of lessons to be learnt.

Hurricane in Algeria

'We arrived on 15th January at Stora, where we had to unload a considerable number of artillery pieces. The vessel was directed by the harbourmaster to the most convenient anchorage for the purpose.

'Doubled anchors were put out from the cathead, one with 100 fathoms of chain, and the other with 80, in a depth of 10 to 11 fathoms. The starboard watch-anchor, backed by a light kedge, was put out from the port quarter to act as a swing preventer; it had a scope of 80 fathoms. Two warps joined end to end, made fast to the rocks at the edge of the beach, held us to starboard. Thus was our fourfold mooring disposed. When it was finished, the topgallant masts were sent down and the unloading commenced.

'During the day of the 21st, a swell appeared on the sea, and the weather took on a threatening aspect: the bar[ometer] fell to 27.6 inches, and the wi[nd] blew in violent squalls from the NE [to] the NNE, then N, then NW. The s[well] continued to rise, and I ordered [the] port watch-anchor to be laid out as [a] precaution, the chains to be veered [to] allow them to work, and at the sa[me] time some slack to be allowed in [the] warps, which the ground swell w[as] sorely straining.

'During that evening of the 21[st] many commercial vessels signalled f[or] help: our spare anchors and so[me] warps were sent off to them; so[me] crews abandoned their own vessels a[nd] sought refuge aboard the Marne. [We] struck our topmasts: the lower yar[ds] were secured. We were holding perfe[ct]ly in spite of the prodigious size of [the] swell, which had already driven tw[o] vessels ashore.

'On the 22nd, at 10 o'clock in t[he] evening, the port chain parted, but t[he] cable and the second chain held us.

168

'On the 23rd and 24th, the weather appeared to improve: the sea moderated, and we were able to drag for, and recover, the broken chain, working the Grapnels from a brig anchored ahead of us. By the morning of the 25th we were able to reshackle the chain, and set it working with the others.

'A few hours after this operation was completed, the weather became atrocious. The Gulf of Stora was now nothing but a mass of breakers from which monstrous waves issued to burst upon the anchorage. I had the hatches of the deck and the battery battened down; the boats in the davits and some of the men were carried away by the seas which were breaking green over the bows as far aft as her foremast. Twenty vessels were smashed to pieces on the shore; three others, moored near to us, foundered at their anchors. The port chain parted; we began to drag, albeit slowly. As a precautionary measure I had had the end of the stern cable led to the bows. I had the stoppers that held it to the stern cut, hoping to claw to windward and, by sheeting in the mizzen to take advantage of the squalls, hold the vessel between the waves of the open sea and the undertow from the land, and avoid the breakers which were now only a short distance away. The hope was vain: nothing could resist the seas which overmastered us. At thirty minutes past two we struck: our position was desperate.

'I called together the officers, the harbourmaster, the sailing master and some captains who had come aboard for refuge some time before, to hear their opinion. Their unanimous advice, which accorded with my own view, was to pay out all the cables to avoid touching the rocks of Pointe Noire, and seek to beach the vessel in the most easily reached bay, which was situated to the south of the breakers on which we had just seen a cargo ship break up and disappear in less than ten minutes. We were fortunate enough to succeed, and the Marne, after a number of terrible concussions, came to her end on a bank of firm sand mixed with rocks about forty fathoms from the shore. . . . We have lost forty-two men, among whom are the surgeon-major, the administration officer, ensign Karche, and my second-in-command, first lieutenant Dagorn, an officer of rare merit, whose loss will make itself felt in my heart for a long time. . . .

'Twenty-four vessels broken up on the coast at Stora and three more foundered at anchor bear sufficient witness to the weather we experienced, which I can compare with nothing that I have seen during all my years in the Navy.'

Conversion charts

kg	0	1	2	3	4	5	6	7	8	9
	lb									
0		2.21	4.41	6.61	8.82	11.02	13.23	15.43	17.64	19
10	22.05	24.25	26.46	28.66	30.86	33.07	35.27	37.47	39.68	41
20	44.09	46.3	48.5	50.71	52.91	55.12	57.32	59.52	61.73	63
30	66.14	68.34	70.55	72.75	74.96	77.16	79.37	81.57	83.78	85
40	88.18	90.39	92.59	94.8	97.0	99.2	101.41	103.61	105.82	108
50	110.23	112.44	114.64	116.85	119.05	121.25	123.46	125.66	127.87	130
60	132.28	134.48	136.69	138.89	141.1	143.3	145.51	147.71	149.91	152
70	154.32	156.53	158.73	160.94	163.14	165.35	167.55	169.76	171.96	174
80	176.37	178.57	180.78	182.98	185.19	187.39	189.6	191.8	194.01	196
90	198.42	200.62	202.83	205.03	207.24	209.44	211.64	213.85	216.05	218
100	220.46	222.67	224.87	227.08	229.28	231.49	233.69	235.9	238.1	240
110	242.51	244.71	246.92	249.12	251.33	253.53	255.74	257.94	260.15	262
120	264.56	266.76	268.96	271.17	273.37	275.58	277.78	279.99	282.19	284
130	286.6	288.81	291.01	293.22	295.42	297.62	299.83	302.03	304.24	306
140	308.65	310.85	313.06	315.26	317.47	319.67	321.88	324.08	326.28	328
150	330.69	332.9	335.1	337.31	339.51	341.72	343.92	346.13	348.33	350
160	352.74	354.94	357.15	359.35	361.56	363.76	365.97	368.17	370.38	372
170	374.79	377.0	379.2	381.4	383.6	385.81	388.01	390.22	392.42	394
180	396.83	399.04	401.24	403.45	405.65	407.86	410.06	412.26	414.47	416
190	418.88	421.08	423.29	425.49	427.68	429.9	432.11	434.31	436.52	438
200	440.93	443.13	445.33	447.54	449.74	451.95	454.15	456.36	458.56	460
210	462.97	465.18	467.38	469.59	471.79	473.99	476.2	478.4	480.61	482
220	485.02	487.22	489.43	491.63	493.84	496.04	498.25	500.45	502.65	504
230	507.06	509.2	511.47	513.6	515.88	518.0	520.29	522.4	524.7	526
240	529.1	531.31	533.5	535.72	537.9	540.13	542.3	544.54	546.7	548
250	551.16	553.36	555.57	557.77	559.97	562.18	564.38	566.59	568.79	571
260	573.2	575.41	577.61	579.82	582.02	584.23	586.43	588.63	590.84	593
270	595.25	597.45	599.66	601.86	604.07	606.27	608.48	610.68	612.89	615
280	617.29	619.5	621.7	623.91	626.11	628.32	630.52	632.73	634.93	637
290	639.34	641.55	643.75	645.95	648.16	650.36	652.57	654.77	656.98	659
300	661.39	663.59	665.8	668.0	670.21	672.41	674.62	676.82	679.02	681
310	683.43	685.64	687.84	690.05	692.25	694.46	696.66	698.87	701.07	703
320	705.48	707.68	709.89	712.09	714.3	716.5	718.71	720.91	723.12	725
330	727.53	729.73	731.93	734.14	736.34	738.55	740.75	742.96	745.16	747
340	749.57	751.78	753.98	756.19	758.39	760.6	762.8	765.0	767.21	769
350	771.62	773.82	776.03	778.23	780.44	782.64	784.85	787.05	789.26	791
360	793.66	795.87	798.07	800.28	802.48	804.69	806.89	809.1	811.31	813
370	815.71	817.92	820.12	822.32	824.53	826.73	828.94	831.14	833.35	835
380	837.76	839.96	842.17	844.37	846.58	848.78	850.98	853.19	855.39	857
390	859.8	862.0	864.21	866.41	868.62	870.8	873.03	875.2	877.44	879
400	881.85	884.05	886.26	888.46	890.67	892.87	895.08	897.28	899.49	901
410	903.9	906.1	908.31	910.51	912.71	914.92	917.12	919.33	921.53	923
420	925.94	928.15	930.35	932.56	934.76	936.97	939.17	941.37	943.58	945
430	947.99	950.19	952.4	954.6	956.81	959.01	961.22	963.42	965.63	967
440	970.03	972.24	974.44	976.65	978.85	981.06	983.26	985.47	987.67	989
450	992.08	994.29	996.49	998.69	1 000.9	1 003.1	1 005.31	1 007.51	1 009.72	1 011
460	1 014.13	1 016.33	1 018.54	1 020.74	1 022.94	1 025.15	1 027.35	1 029.56	1 031.76	1 033
470	1 036.17	1 038.38	1 040.58	1 042.79	1 044.99	1 047.2	1 049.4	1 051.6	1 053.81	1 056
480	1 058.22	1 060.42	1 062.63	1 064.83	1 067.04	1 069.24	1 071.45	1 073.65	1 075.86	1 078.
490	1 080.27	1 082.47	1 084.67	1 086.88	1 089.08	1 091.29	1 093.49	1 095.7	1 097.9	1 100
500	1 102.31									

nds to kilograms

0	1	2	3	4	5	6	7	8	9
kg									
	0.45	0.91	1.36	1.81	2.27	2.72	3.18	3.63	4.08
4.54	4.99	5.44	5.9	6.35	6.8	7.26	7.71	8.16	8.62
9.07	9.53	9.98	10.43	10.89	11.34	11.79	12.25	12.7	13.15
13.61	14.06	14.52	14.97	15.42	15.88	16.33	16.78	17.24	17.69
18.14	18.6	19.05	19.5	19.96	20.41	20.87	21.32	21.77	22.23
22.68	23.13	23.59	24.04	24.49	24.95	25.4	25.85	26.31	26.76
27.22	27.67	28.12	28.58	29.03	29.48	29.94	30.39	30.84	31.3
31.75	32.21	32.66	33.11	33.57	34.02	34.47	34.93	35.38	35.83
36.29	36.74	37.19	37.65	38.1	38.56	39.01	39.46	39.92	40.37
40.82	41.28	41.73	42.18	42.64	43.09	43.54	44.0	44.45	44.91
45.36	45.81	46.27	46.72	47.17	47.63	48.08	48.53	48.99	49.44
49.9	50.35	50.8	51.26	51.71	52.16	52.62	53.07	53.52	53.98
54.43	54.88	55.34	55.79	56.25	56.7	57.15	57.61	58.06	58.51
58.97	59.42	59.87	60.33	60.78	61.24	61.69	62.14	62.6	63.05
63.5	63.96	64.41	64.86	65.32	65.77	66.22	66.68	67.13	67.59
68.04	68.49	68.95	69.4	69.85	70.31	70.76	71.21	71.67	72.12
72.57	73.03	73.48	73.94	74.39	74.84	75.3	75.75	76.2	76.66
77.11	77.56	78.02	78.47	78.93	79.38	79.83	80.29	80.74	81.19
81.65	82.1	82.55	83.01	83.46	83.91	84.37	84.82	85.28	85.73
86.18	86.64	87.09	87.54	88.0	88.45	88.9	89.36	89.81	90.26
90.72	91.17	91.63	92.08	92.53	92.99	93.44	93.89	94.35	94.8
95.25	95.71	96.16	96.62	97.07	97.52	97.98	98.43	98.88	99.34
99.79	100.24	100.7	101.15	101.61	102.06	102.51	102.97	103.42	103.87
104.33	104.78	105.23	105.69	106.14	106.59	107.05	107.5	107.96	108.41
108.86	109.32	109.77	110.22	110.68	111.13	111.58	112.04	112.49	112.95
113.4	113.85	114.31	114.76	115.21	115.67	116.12	116.57	117.03	117.48
117.93	118.39	118.84	119.3	119.75	120.2	120.66	121.11	121.56	122.02
122.47	122.92	123.38	123.83	124.28	124.74	125.19	125.65	126.1	126.55
127.01	127.46	127.91	128.37	128.82	129.27	129.73	130.18	130.64	131.09
131.54	132.0	132.45	132.9	133.36	133.81	134.26	134.72	135.17	135.62
136.08	136.53	136.99	137.44	137.89	138.35	138.8	139.25	139.71	140.16
140.61	141.07	141.52	141.97	142.43	142.88	143.34	143.79	144.24	144.7
145.15	145.6	146.06	146.51	146.96	147.42	147.87	148.33	148.78	149.23
149.69	150.14	150.59	151.05	151.5	151.95	152.41	152.86	153.31	153.77
154.22	154.68	155.13	155.58	156.04	156.49	156.94	157.4	157.85	158.3
158.76	159.21	159.67	160.12	160.57	161.03	161.48	161.93	162.39	162.84
163.29	163.75	164.2	164.65	165.11	165.56	166.02	166.47	166.92	167.38
167.83	168.28	168.74	169.1	169.64	170.1	170.55	171.0	171.46	171.91
172.37	172.82	173.27	173.73	174.18	174.63	175.09	175.54	175.99	176.45
176.9	177.36	177.81	178.26	178.72	179.17	179.62	180.08	180.53	180.98
181.44	181.89	182.34	182.8	183.25	183.71	184.16	184.61	185.07	185.52
185.97	186.43	186.88	187.33	187.79	188.24	188.69	189.15	189.6	190.06
190.51	190.96	191.42	191.87	192.32	192.78	193.23	193.68	194.14	194.59
195.05	195.5	195.95	196.41	196.86	197.31	197.77	198.22	198.67	199.13
199.58	200.03	200.49	200.94	201.4	201.85	202.3	202.76	203.21	203.66
204.12	204.57	205.02	205.48	205.93	206.39	206.84	207.29	207.75	208.2
208.65	209.11	209.56	210.01	210.47	210.92	211.37	211.83	212.28	212.74
213.19	213.64	214.1	214.55	215.0	215.46	215.91	216.36	216.82	217.27
217.72	218.18	218.63	219.09	219.54	219.99	220.45	220.9	221.35	221.81
222.26	222.71	223.17	223.62	224.08	224.53	224.98	225.44	225.89	226.34
226.8									

m	0	1	2	3	4	5	6	7	8	9
	ft									
0		3.28	6.56	9.84	13.12	16.40	19.69	22.97	26.25	29
10	32.8	36.09	39.37	42.65	45.93	49.21	52.49	55.77	59.06	62
20	65.62	68.9	72.17	75.45	78.74	82.02	85.3	88.58	91.86	95.
30	98.43	101.7	104.99	108.27	111.55	114.82	118.11	121.39	124.67	127
40	131.23	134.51	137.8	141.08	144.36	147.63	150.91	154.2	157.48	160.
50	164.04	167.32	170.6	173.89	177.17	180.45	183.73	187.01	190.29	193.
60	196.85	200.13	203.41	206.69	209.97	213.25	216.54	219.82	223.1	226.
70	229.66	232.94	236.22	239.5	242.78	246.06	249.34	252.63	255.91	259.
80	262.46	265.75	269.03	272.31	275.59	278.87	282.15	285.43	288.71	292.
90	295.28	298.56	301.84	305.12	308.4	311.68	314.96	318.24	321.52	324.
100	328.08	331.37	334.65	337.93	341.21	344.49	347.77	351.05	354.33	357.
110	360.89	364.17	367.45	370.74	374.02	377.3	380.58	383.86	387.14	390.
120	393.7	396.98	400.26	403.54	406.82	410.1	413.39	416.67	419.95	423.
130	426.51	429.79	433.07	436.35	439.63	442.91	446.19	449.48	452.76	456.
140	459.32	462.6	465.88	469.16	472.44	475.72	479.0	482.28	485.56	488.
150	492.13	495.41	498.69	502.0	505.25	508.53	511.81	515.09	518.37	521.
160	524.93	528.22	531.5	534.78	538.06	541.34	544.62	547.9	551.18	554.
170	557.74	561.02	564.3	567.59	570.87	574.15	577.43	580.71	583.99	587.
180	590.55	593.83	597.11	600.39	603.68	606.96	610.24	613.52	616.8	620.
190	623.36	626.64	629.92	633.2	636.48	639.76	643.05	646.33	649.6	652.
200	656.17	659.45	662.73	666.01	669.29	672.57	675.85	679.13	682.42	685.
210	688.98	692.26	695.54	698.82	702.1	705.38	708.66	711.94	715.22	718.
220	721.79	725.07	728.35	731.63	734.91	738.19	741.47	744.75	748.03	751.
230	754.59	757.87	761.16	764.44	767.72	771.0	774.28	777.56	780.84	784.
240	787.4	790.68	793.96	797.24	800.53	803.81	807.09	810.37	813.65	816.
250	820.21									

ft	0	1	2	3	4	5	6	7	8	9
	m									
0		0.31	0.6	0.91	1.22	1.52	1.83	2.13	2.44	2.
10	3.05	3.35	3.66	3.96	4.27	4.57	4.88	5.18	5.49	5.
20	6.1	6.4	6.71	7.01	7.31	7.62	7.92	8.23	8.53	8.
30	9.14	9.45	9.75	10.06	10.36	10.67	10.97	11.28	11.58	11.
40	12.19	12.5	12.80	13.1	13.41	13.72	14.02	14.36	14.63	14.
50	15.24	15.54	15.85	16.15	16.46	16.76	17.07	17.37	17.68	17.
60	18.29	18.59	18.9	19.2	19.58	19.81	20.12	20.42	20.73	21.
70	21.33	21.64	21.95	22.25	22.56	22.86	23.16	23.47	23.77	24.
80	24.38	24.69	24.99	25.3	25.6	25.91	26.21	26.52	26.82	27.
90	27.43	27.74	28.04	28.35	28.65	28.96	29.26	29.57	29.87	30.
100	30.48	30.78	31.09	31.39	31.7	32.0	32.31	32.61	32.92	33.
110	33.53	33.83	34.14	34.44	34.75	35.05	35.37	35.67	36.0	36.
120	36.58	36.88	37.19	37.49	37.8	38.1	38.41	38.7	39.01	39.
130	39.62	39.93	40.23	40.54	40.84	41.15	41.45	41.76	42.06	42.
140	42.67	42.98	43.28	43.59	43.89	44.2	44.5	44.81	45.11	45.
150	45.72	46.02	46.33	46.63	46.94	47.24	47.55	47.85	48.16	48.
160	48.77	49.07	49.38	49.68	49.99	50.29	50.6	50.9	51.21	51.
170	51.82	52.12	52.43	52.73	53.04	53.34	53.64	53.95	54.25	54.
180	54.86	55.17	55.47	55.78	56.08	56.39	56.69	57.0	57.3	57.
190	57.91	58.22	58.52	58.83	59.13	59.44	59.74	60.05	60.35	60.
200	60.96	61.26	61.57	61.87	62.18	62.48	62.79	63.09	63.4	63.
210	64.01	64.31	64.62	64.92	65.23	65.53	65.84	66.14	66.45	66.
220	67.06	67.36	67.67	67.97	68.28	68.58	68.89	69.19	69.49	69.
230	70.1	70.41	70.71	71.02	71.32	71.63	71.93	72.24	72.54	72.
240	73.15	73.46	73.76	74.07	74.37	74.68	74.98	75.29	75.59	75.
250	76.2									

PE SIZES: CONVERSION TO METRIC

DIAMETER in	DIAMETER mm	CIRCUMFERENCE in
1/16	1.5 mm	3/16
1/12	2 mm	1/4
1/8	3 mm	3/8
5/32	4 mm	1/2
3/16	5 mm	5/8
7/32	6 mm	3/4
1/4	7 mm	7/8
5/16	8 mm	1 in
3/8	9 mm	1 1/8
7/16	10 mm	1 1/4
1/2	12 mm	1 1/2
9/16	14 mm	1 3/4
5/8	16 mm	2 in
3/4	18 mm	2 1/4
13/16	20 mm	2 1/2
1	24 mm	3 in

ASUREMENT OF ROPE SIZES

he UK, rope used to be sold measured in
es **circumference**. Nowadays it is sold in **mm**
eter. In the USA, however, it is sold in **inches**
eter.

CHAIN

In the UK, chain is still mostly sold in inches diameter, as in the USA. However, the metric equivalents are as follows:

in	mm
1/4	6.3
5/16	8
3/8	9.5
7/16	11.1
1/2	12.7
9/16	14
5/8	16
3/4	19
7/8	22
1	25.5